Finding Safe Harbor in Retirement

*Strategies to help you navigate
the seas of financial uncertainty
and stay afloat throughout retirement*

Finding Safe Harbor in Retirement

Strategies to help you navigate the seas of financial uncertainty and stay afloat throughout retirement

By James D. Stillman

Copyright ©2014 by Jim Stillman

All rights reserved. No part of this book may be used or reproduced in any manner whatsoever, without express written permission, except for brief quotations for use in reviews or critical articles.

Table of Contents

Foreword

Preface

Chapter 1: The Baby Boom Generation Comes of Age 1

Chapter 2: No Fumbling in the Red Zone 11

Chapter 3: Common *Myth*-stakes Retirees Make 25

Chapter 4: The Three Money Worlds 33

Chapter 5: Putting Your Financial Ship in Order 41

Chapter 6: Planning the Risk Out of Retirement 49

Chapter 7: The Case for Seeking Professional Financial Advice 65

Chapter 8: Steering Clear of Hidden Retirement Dangers 71

Chapter 9: How Much Liquidity Do You Really
Need in Retirement? 82

Chapter 10: Taking a Fresh Look at Life Insurance and Annuities 93

Chapter 11: Smooth Sailing Through The Golden Years 107

Afterword 114

About the Author 117

Dedication 120

Acknowledgements 121

Foreword

By Ty Stillman

I ended up working for my father, Jim Stillman, out of mutual necessity. I graduated from Rutgers University in the spring of 2010, right around when Dad was looking to expand his practice. I needed a job; he needed some help running things and keeping an even keel on the extra demands with which he had been presented. It was daunting for us both at first, but we found our footing pretty quickly.

If you're already a friend or client of Jim Stillman, then you know how much he values keeping his business very focused, and family-based. I was with him for two years out of school, but my sister, Kelly, has since taken on my old post (and run fantastically with it, frankly). Many of his peers operate much larger practices with many, many more employees, but Jim's desire has always been to keep it close to him and maintain a familiar and comfortable environment for the families he helps day in and day out.

One thing I learned very quickly while working with Dad was this. He's very passionate about his work, and is on a mission to educate those planning for retirement. It's hard to argue with the results.

In those two years, I got to observe my father do what he does firsthand instead of only hearing about it. I also learned plenty about the intricacies of financial planning, and I could still elaborate on them if asked to, but I figure this book will do a better job of that than I could ever hope to. The more important things to share are the small things I observed over those two years.

Dad displays an untiring work ethic. He'd be at the office late to work on something so often that I just stopped keeping track of it. He will take his notes and laptop out with him to lunch, or on Lake

Norman over the weekend – time meant to be for relaxation – to keep working on a financial plan or an outline for a presentation.

He works incredibly hard to keep educating himself, constantly absorbing all the material he can in order to stay up to date with (and ahead of) trends in financial markets. When he jokes that he's far from the sharpest knife in the drawer (I jokingly agree, and will for the rest of my life), but I came to see that he's far more clever and intelligent than he gives himself credit for. Whatever **perceived** deficiencies he has in that department are solidly filled in by the work he puts in learning as much as he can so that he can better assist his clients. Dad always says, "Your attitude, determines your aptitude".

The business itself may be a small family practice, but in truth it's a *very* large family. Dad cares deeply about his clients and considers them part of his extended family. He gives an extremely personal touch to every case he takes on, and his clients value that because it's not something often found in financial planning. It goes a long way in making people feel comfortable with the decisions they need to make with what often amounts to their life's savings.

I'm proud of those two years I worked with my father, and I'm proud that a lot of the concepts and strategies that I helped him refine are finally making it to print. Jim will walk you through, in detail, financial planning concepts like the "Rule of 100" and the "Three Money Worlds." He'll talk about the benefits of annuity-based planning for retirement, and why mutual funds aren't always the best investment option for retirees. He'll even discuss *why* it's important to have professional help in planning your finances, among many other things.

My father has a lifetime of experience and experiences: He was a star running back, swimmer, and track athlete for his Milwaukee high school. He's an ace bowler (ask him about the few thousand bucks he won in a bowling tournament back in 1974, and how he used the money to completely pay off his first car, or the 279 game he dropped on my head fairly recently at age 60). He brokered deals with big movie studios on prototype VHS cover art during his time in the printing industry (check out the original 3D video sleeve for *Independence Day* if you've still got it sitting around somewhere). He is a practiced sailor, and avid boater. You'll see in this book that he draws on all these experiences to deliver financial advice in an easy-to-understand, common sense manner. He is all of the things I just talked about, but he's also an incredible financial planner with over fifteen years of experience to draw upon, and he never stops learning. Perhaps most importantly, he is an incredible father that my sister and I are fortunate to have, along with our mother Judy, Jim's wife of more than 30+ years.

    If you're already a client or friend of dad's, I know it'll be useful to again see so many of the strategies that he's discussed with you over the months or years. If you're only getting to know him, know that what follows is only the tip of the iceberg. I hope you will find all you are about to read valuable and illuminating, but please know that there's so much more still buried in that head of Dad's.

Preface

    As a sailor and experienced boater for more than 40 years, I have learned that anything can happen on the water. Expecting the unexpected is the rule of the sea, and plans need to be in place for almost any event. One minute you can be cruising along, enjoying a perfect 12-knot breeze on smooth water with the sun on your face, and the next minute you can find yourself aground on a sandbar. There is no feeling more sickening while sailing than the sudden lurching stop as your keel finds one of those hidden mounds that lurk just a few feet below the surface of the water. The bow dips, the stern comes up, and anything not tightly secured down below goes flying. What you thought was open water - and it may have even been marked that way on the nautical chart - was not.

    The water along the North Carolina shoreline, which used to be one of my favorite sailing spots, is quite shallow until you get offshore a little ways. Big ships and sailing vessels pay close attention to the day markers and buoys that line the channels where the water is deep enough for them to pass. Unfortunately, when hurricanes, tides, and nor'easters come through, the sands beneath the surface can and will shift on a daily basis. These new hazards do not show up on the charts and are often discovered the hard way by unsuspecting skippers.

    These days, cruising sailboats and yachts come equipped with transponders – a device that measures the distance from the bottom of your hull to the ocean floor below.

    These devices are commonly known as depth sounders. In the shoal-laden waters of the east coast, with its necklace of barrier islands, these devices are essential navigational aids and it's always a good idea to keep a sharp eye on the readings they produce. Unless you are in the center of the channel, which is routinely dredged for safety, running aground is a real threat.

    As a Registered Financial Consultant and financial planner, I have often contemplated how much alike sailing treacherous waters is to the managing of our personal finances, especially when we approach retirement. We may have worked hard and saved hard all of our lives only to experience financial shipwreck because of hazards that can suddenly take us unawares. Even a vessel with the best and most modern electronic navigational equipment can run afoul due to a sudden storm or unseen obstruction. Likewise, even the most prudent investor can experience trouble if he or she isn't vigilant.

One of the reasons I decided to write this book is to put in public forum certain principles that I have been sharing with clients for decades - principles that will enable investors and retirement savers to relax and enjoy their lives when it is time to retire, not pace the floor at night wondering about the status of their finances, and whether they are going to have enough money to see them through their golden years.

A few years ago, immediately after the market crash of 2008-2009, a couple sat in my office and told me with somber expressions how they had lost more than half of their life savings - just when they could least afford it, right after they'd retired.

"We just didn't see it coming," said the brokenhearted man. "Our broker didn't warn us that such a thing could happen to us. We thought we had made it clear we could not afford to lose our money, and we needed it for income during retirement."

"We were continually told not to worry because we were 'diversified.'" Diversified into what, his wife asked, obviously hurt and frustrated. "If we had had some advance warning…if we had known we were taking on so much risk, maybe we would have been okay. We were not in a position to lose that much money, so why did we?"

Sometimes lessons are learned the hard way. Unfortunately this story repeats itself far too often. People don't "plan to fail", they "fail to plan" *properly* for retirement. Please remember, Wall Street does not have all the answers! Many times that's the biggest problem. At some point in life, it's not how much you *make;* it's how much you *keep* of what you make. Wall Street simply carries too much risk for most retirees. It's not that you *shouldn't* invest using Wall Street strategies in retirement; it's about *how much* you invest.

Since I specialize almost exclusively in the area of financial planning for those who are either approaching retirement or who have just retired, none of my clients lost money in the aforementioned Wall Street catastrophe. Like a safe harbor in an offshore storm, the principles of safe money investing protected them and preserved their assets. The couple mentioned above was forced to alter their plans for retirement. I had to deliver the bad news to them that the math of their new financial situation after the stock market losses simply would not support the early retirement they were hoping for. They figured the only way to make up what they had lost was to reduce income, work part time, and try and save more money in a safe place. Even then, they were concerned about whether they would have enough to last them the rest of their lives. In the back of their minds were lingering doubts about long term care and other possible eventualities that could knock them off course or place them as a burden on their families in their old age. Of course, we are doing everything possible to get them back on track for the happy retirement they are wishing for. But the point remains – they should never have been in that position of risk in the first place. Shame on their big shot Wall Street advisor who did not treat their money with the respect it deserved!

As you read this book, it is my wish that you do so with an open mind when it comes to strategies and concepts you will see explored and explained. Some of the views expressed here may be new to you. Don't discount them because they have not been widely advertised. There may also be techniques of investing and methods of money management that don't necessarily fit the "mainstream" thinking of the Wall Street crowd. I can't apologize for advocating what works. I also cannot in good conscience suggest ineffective investing ideas as sound thinking when I know them to be dangerous to those contemplating retirement. That would be like a meteorologist altering a storm warning just to be popular with picnickers and boaters! To the contrary, in the following pages, I intend to pull back the curtain and show you the good, the bad, and the not-so-pretty, working on the assumption that you agree with me that knowledge is better than ignorance in virtually every endeavor we may undertake – especially when our money is involved. Please remember, knowledge by itself is not enough when it comes to retirement planning. But, applied knowledge is powerful!

If you have read this far, you may have gathered that I enjoy making my points with sailing and boating metaphors and illustrations about the water. This is no accident. When I was 31, my wife, Judy, and I "retired" and spent a year or two living on a 35-foot sailboat, cruising the Great Lakes, the east coast, the Florida Keys and the Bahamas. It taught us many things at an early age. Those lessons still influence us today. When I founded JDS Enterprizes Inc. in 2003, and JDS Wealth Management Corp. in 2008, I quickly learned that education plus common sense is "job one" in financial planning. Just as knowing where you are on the water is essential before you can plot a course to your destination, plotting a financial destination starts with knowing and understanding where you are now. Next comes having a clear view of where you want to go. Connecting those two dots – where you are now and where you want to be – involves both the skill and science of navigation. As we take that journey together, dear reader, it is my hope that you will find the information presented here rewarding, useful and interesting.

Chapter One

The Baby Boom Generation Comes of Age

"Today there are about 40 million retirees receiving benefits; by the time all the baby boomers have retired, there will be more than 72 million retirees drawing Social Security benefits." ~ Tony Snow

World War II had just ended. American soldiers who had just saved the world for democracy were returning home by the thousands to cheering crowds and ticker tape parades. The factories that had been making tanks and airplanes were retooling to manufacture consumer goods that were now in great demand. Many of the women who had operated the machines at those factories were turning in their hard hats and I.D. badges and returning to domestic life. The young men who had gone to war now wanted to settle down at home and raise families. As they reintegrated into civilian life, the birth rate jumped dramatically. In 1946, live births in the U.S. surged from 222,721 in January to 339,499 in October. By the end of the 1940s, about 32 million babies had been born, compared with 24 million in the 1930s. In 1954, annual births first topped four million and did not drop below that figure until 1965, when four out of 10 Americans were under the age of 20. It was called the great "Baby Boom." Officially, anyone born between the years of 1946 and 1964 is part of the baby boom generation – a group that would have, and is still having, the greatest social and economic impact on American life than any generation in history.

In the years after the war, couples who could not afford families during the Great Depression made up for lost time; the mood was now optimistic. During the war unemployment ended and the economy greatly expanded; afterwards the country experienced vigorous economic growth until the 1970s. Toward the end of World War II, congress passed the G.I. Bill of Rights. This bill encouraged home ownership and investment in higher education through the distribution of loans at low or no interest rates to veterans. Servicemen in record numbers began to attend college. This led to higher incomes and home ownership. Even when you adjust for inflation, the baby boom generation has earned and continues to earn more than any generation before it.

What's happening now is those babies are turning 65 and looking at retirement. Yep, the generation that brought us the Beatles, The Rolling Stones and put a man on the moon is now eyeing retirement square in the face. The generation that came up with "Rock Around the Clock" and "Never trust anyone over 30," is now lining up for Medicare and Social Security and talking about their "Golden Years." The kids who grew up wearing Davy Crocket coonskin caps and watching black and white TV, lived through the hippie movement, went from beads and bell bottoms to board rooms and BMW's, and presided over the arms race, the space race and the rat race, are now (who would have thunk it?) senior citizens. If you think this phenomenon is having a dramatic socio-economic effect on the world, you are right. Simply by the sheer force of their numbers, baby boomers are still shaping the world around us. Some observers of the world scene say that boomers are turning 65 at the rate of 10,000 per day for the next 18 – 20 years. Is this senior stampede ready for retirement?

Demographer Philip Longman, in his white paper *Why Are So Many Baby Boomers Ill Prepared for Retirement?*, says that boomers get high marks for **earning** money but poor marks when it comes to **saving** it. Unlike their parents' generation, boomers grew up in a consumer's paradise awash with fancy cars, color televisions, electronic gadgets and toys of all types. They had no memory of hard times and soup kitchens, so, as a culture, saving for a rainy day was just not in their generational chip. To make matters worse, the credit card was born just in time to accommodate the buying spree. What cash couldn't buy the plastic could, regardless of the budget and high interest rates. Boomers were great consumers. They still are. But now a lot of them are worried about having enough to live on in retirement.

A poll conducted by the Associated Press* in 2011 found that 89 percent of the 77 million people born between 1946 and 1964 are not strongly convinced they will be able to live in comfort in their later years. One in four said they don't think they will ever be able to retire. The 2011 poll was taken four years after the housing bubble burst in 2007 and three years after the stock market collapse of 2008. These seismic economic events left boomers even more worried about their retirement future. Six in 10 said their investments, retirement plans, and home equities lost significant value, resulting in 42 percent of those surveyed declaring that they were for being forced to delay retirement

"I worry about an emergency," Nina Scott, 56 years old and a teacher in Boston, told ABC News, who reported on the poll shortly after it was taken. "I worry about healthcare…"

* *The AP-LifeGoesStrong.com poll was conducted from March 4-13, 2011 by Knowledge Networks of Menlo Park, Calif., and involved online interviews with 1,160 baby boomers born between 1946 and 1964. The margin of sampling error is plus or minus 3.5 percentage points.*

Pensions Are Disappearing

There was a time when American employees could count on a pension when they retired. Employers wanted workers to stay with them, so they offered, as part of their benefit package, a defined benefit pension program that promised to pay them a salary for the rest of their lives when they retired. It was a true benefit. The employee was not required to contribute to the program. The reason why we speak of these programs in the past tense is because they are almost extinct these days. They have been replaced by 401(k) or similar programs that are known as defined ***contribution*** plans instead of defined ***benefit*** plans. Companies will sometimes match a portion of what the employees contribute to these retirement programs, but it is up to employees to carve out a portion of their paycheck each week to provide for their own retirement. Even then, the payout is not guaranteed. These retirement programs are typically invested in mutual funds and are subject to the rise and fall of the stock market for growth. During the 1990's, when the stock market was roaring, qualified retirement programs such as 401(k) and 403(b) plans could do no wrong. But many of these plans went backwards in the 2000s, just when baby boomers saw retirement beginning to loom large on the horizon. As if these concerns aren't enough, rising fuel costs, higher health care costs and declining property values are, at the time of this writing, causing once confident baby boomers to be more and more uncertain of their financial futures.

A USA Today/Gallup Poll taken in early 2012 said that two-thirds of baby boomers say they are less optimistic about retirement than they were 10 years ago. The Insured Retirement Institute recently surveyed a cross-section of individuals from 50 to 66 years of age, and found that only 40 percent of them were confident of having enough to cover basic expenses in retirement. Sixty percent believed that their retirement security would be worse than that of their parents. Even the pollsters were surprised at how much the pendulum of public opinion within this group had swung toward the negative in just 10 years.

According to Annamaria Lusardi, economics professor at the George Washington University School of Business, many Americans just choose not to worry about it. She points out that there is a general lack of financial literacy and planning among "a sizable group of the population that has not even thought about retirement." She points out that many people see retirement as a distant stage of their lives even if it's only five years away. The 2011 AP survey said that 64 percent of boomers polled said they see Social Security as the main source of their retirement income.

Why Is Longevity A Concern?

Americans are living longer. You sometimes hear people say that 60 is the new 40. They aren't too far off. In 1940, the life expectancy of a 65-year-old was almost 14 years; today it is more than 20 years. Question: What could be sweeter news than to hear that you are likely to live a long time? Answer: To hear that you will also have enough money to see you through those extra years.

Death may be frightening, but to a majority of older Americans, the possibility of outliving their savings is even worse, according to a 2010 poll taken by Allianz Life Insurance Co. of North America. Among people ages 44-75, the survey revealed that more than three in five (61 percent) said they fear depleting their assets more than they fear dying. The poll also found that 92 percent of the 3,257 people polled agreed that the United States is facing a crisis in its retirement system. Among those ages 44 to 54, some 56 percent are afraid they won't be able to cover their basic living expenses in retirement. And 36 percent said they had no idea whether their nest egg was sufficient. More than half (53 percent) said their net worth dropped significantly during the 2008 economic downturn. Of those, virtually all said they have cut back on such things as entertaining and dining out.

How Quickly We Forget

I read recently where psychologists at the University of California-Santa Cruz discovered that when adults remember things, they tend to hold onto the positive and slough off the negative. This little trick of memory distortion is what allows baseball players to remember how to hit pitches and forget the misses. I suppose you can call it positive thinking, and I guess it is a good thing that keeps us looking forward with confidence instead of fear.

One example of this is how quickly people forget the devastating effects of hurricanes. North Carolina, the state where I live, seems to be a magnet for these storms. Referring to the bulge of the Outer Banks as it protrudes into the Atlantic, some say that North Carolina "has its chin stuck out," as if daring the storms of summer and early fall to hit it. As a consequence, several hurricanes have taken the dare and blasted the NC coast over the years. At the time of this writing, the state has been hit by more than 400 known tropical storms since record-keeping started, costing 1,000 lives and doing $11 billion in damage. According to the N.C. Climate Office, an estimated 17.5 percent of all North Atlantic hurricanes have affected the state, making it the fourth most hurricane-prone state in the nation behind Florida, Texas and Louisiana. Still, in the face of the statistics, people can't seem to resist building houses on every inch of sandy soil available to them along North Carolina's 301-mile shoreline. I remember seeing the aerial video images of the southern N.C. coast after Hurricane Fran, which hit in September 1996. Topsail Beach, a favorite vacation spot just north of Wilmington, North Carolina, was virtually wiped away. The coastal building boom that had transpired during the 1970s and 1980s had left very few vacant Oceanside lots. After Fran, there were plenty. You would think people would be afraid to build there again. And for a while, they were. But how quickly we forget! Ten years after the storm, the destroyed homes on this flat, dune-less stretch of sand were rebuilt and the population of the Topsail Beach actually increased! Many long-time residents of the North Carolina coast know that it just a matter of time before the windy fist of another hurricane gives Topsail Beach another punch in the face and the cycle of forgetting the past can start all over again.

It's like that with economic storms as well. The 1990s were virtually free of economic bad news. In those days the stock market knew only one direction – up! You could throw a dart at the Wall Street big board and buy anything on which the point landed and come out a winner. The nation was in love with the internet. Any company that ended in "dot com" was revered as a sure winner.

Then in March 2000, the foundations of the information technology house of cards began to tremble when some of the "dot coms" with weak fundamentals began to fold. One of the most egregious examples of this boom to bust phenomenon was Pets.com, a company founded on the idea of selling pet supplies over the internet. It began operations in 1998 and was highly advertised, appearing in the 1999 Macy's Day Parade and the 2000 Super Bowl. It's cute little sock puppet mascot was even interviewed by *People* magazine and appeared on television's Good Morning America. Few knew that the company actually lost money on most of its sales. When the San Francisco- based company finally faced the fiscal reality that its business model was a failure, it disappeared quickly from the scene, taking some $300 million of investor money with it. Other companies associated with the World Wide Web began to close up shop. Soon the rush to get out of the over-bought technology stocks began. On March 10, 2000 the NASDAQ composite index peaked at 5,048.62, more than double its value a year before. Then, a number of things began to happen. The overall economy began to show signs of weakening. The U.S. Federal Reserve increased interest rates six times throughout 1999 and early 2000. Microsoft, the world's largest software manufacturer, came under attack by critics claiming it was a monopoly, therefore in violation of antitrust laws. The courts officially agreed with the critics on April 3, 2000. The next day, the NASDAQ fell to 3,649. The bust was in full gear and by 2001 the bubble was deflating at full speed. Investors renamed the dot coms "dot bombs." InfoSpace, an internet-based information services company, was trading at $1,305 per share in March 2000, and at $22 per share by April 2001.

The ensuing stock market crash was severe and widespread. Economists define a bear market as when there is a decline of more than 20 percent in the Standard & Poor's 500 Index. With 20/20 hindsight, market analysts now say that the bear market that followed the bursting of the dot com bubble began in March 2000 and ended in October 2002. It lasted 37 months and resulted in a 49.1 percent decline from which it took 87 months to fully recover. (*Source: www.standardandpoors.com*)

Many people lost fortunes during the 2000 crash. The second half of the 1990s gave a false impression that success was easy because of the exceptional. Investors were getting returns of 20-30 percent. It was hard to convince them that it was too good to be true and that it would eventually collapse on its ears. And just like those homebuilders on the North Carolina shore, investors who fled the market soon returned with the same alacrity and abandon. In 2007/2008 the bottom dropped out again.

The only thing the Wall Street crashes of 2000 and 2008 had in common was the root cause – overconfidence and greed. This time the problem was a housing bubble. People couldn't build houses fast enough. There was almost a feeding frenzy to buy property and build on it. You could drive past the outskirts of virtually any city in America and see the workers putting up new walls and siding. Much of the building was speculative. Loans were easy to obtain. People thought property values would always rise, so banks thought they were covered as long as they had a property as collateral.

Exotic loans that required no proof of employment or income were popping up. Adjustable rate mortgages were the rage. What difference did it make if you never intended to pay back the money? You would just flip the house and move into another one in a few years. Loans called "interest-only" loans were invested, which assumed that none of the principal would ever be repaid – just the interest.

Of course, there were warning signs that this couldn't last. Some alert analysts began sending signals as early as 2006 that trouble was brewing on the horizon, but it was as if no one wanted to hear bad news. Even government agencies, who had the authority to step in and avert disaster, failed to act. One of the first major warning signs came in August 2007, when the Federal Reserve Board, realizing that big banks were overextended, began selling its reserves of Treasury Department securities to add liquidity. In making that move, the government in essence accepted subprime mortgages as collateral.

Still on an upward roll, the Dow ended 2007 at an apparently healthy 13,264. Ordinarily sensitive to bad news, nothing seemed to faze this one until the first of the too-big-to-fail banks, the venerable old Bear Stearns, couldn't hold its breath any longer and declared bankruptcy. Suddenly the news was dominated by a new phrase - "mortgage crisis." The Bear Sterns collapse was followed by news that two of the largest financial institutions associated with mortgages, the Federal National Mortgage Association (Fannie Mae) and the Federal Home Loan Mortgage Corporation (Freddie Mac), were in trouble. The Dow skidded to 11,000. On Monday, September 15, 2008, banking giant Lehman Brothers began coughing red ink and declared bankruptcy. The Dow responded by diving 504 points in one day.

On Wednesday, September 17, 2008, money market funds lost $144 billion and the Dow fell another 449 points in the panic. Twelve days later, on September 29, 2008, the Dow lost a record 777.68 points in one day!. – a new record! The selling stampede was in full swing and the wheels were coming off the Wall Street wagon. The DJIA had hit a low of 7,552 and the Great Recession of 2008 was officially underway. Depending on whose statistics you believe, the U.S. economy lost around $12 trillion. That's *trillion* with a "T" – a number that is hard to wrap our minds around.

Because million rhymes with billion and billion rhymes with trillion, we may not fathom just how much bigger a trillion is from either of its two sound-alike cousins. A million is one thousand thousand. If you write the figure one million, it will be a one followed by six zeros. As numbers go, a million is mentally manageable. If you earned $45,000 per year and saved every penny, you would have $1,000,000 in 22 years. One million ants weigh six pounds. One million dollars divided evenly among the entire population of the U.S. would give everyone about one third of one cent.

Add three zeros to a million and you have a billion. A billion is one thousand million. If you earn $45,000 per year and saved every penny would have a billion dollars in 22,000 years. A billion ants would weigh more than three tons. One billion dollars divided equally among the population of the U.S. would give everyone about $3.33.

After billion comes trillion. Only three more zeros, but what a much bigger number! It's at this point that we start identifying with the Piraha, a forest-dwelling tribe in central Brazil that has no concept of numbers. They can count to two. After that, it's "many." A trillion is one million million (or one thousand billion – take your pick). A trillion ants would weigh 3,000 tons. One trillion dollars divided evenly among the entire population of the U.S. would give every American a little over $3,000.

What's a little scary to me, whether we are talking about the national debt or how much the stock market loses in a recession, is how easily we can let the "T" word slide off our tongues. Academically, it is calculable. But practically, it's just too much to wrap our minds around.

In human terms, the trillions of dollars in losses following the 2008 stock market crash were devastating. I know of several senior citizens who were over exposed in the stock market, lost half their life savings, and had to postpone retirement indefinitely, hoping to recover at least a portion of what they lost. According to some reports, senior citizens lost approximately $2.8 trillion in the 2008 stock market plunge. Their losses were statistically greater because they had accumulated more money. Their losses were more devastating because of the timing. Younger investors still working with time on their side could afford to wait for the market to recover. Older investors, nearing retirement and preparing to snip the umbilical cord connecting them to a weekly paycheck, were forced to rethink their options.

Learning from the Past

Philosopher George Santayana is credited with coining the adage: "Those who cannot learn from history are doomed to repeat it."

The Titanic sank because of overconfidence on a risk-laden sea. Its builders felt that it was unsinkable. Looking back, it seems hard to believe that anyone in 1912 could have believed that 52,000 tons of steel couldn't sink. While the ship's owners and designers never claimed that it was "unsinkable," apparently that was the perception of the general public at the time. It's even in the official record of correspondence associated with that disaster. When the New York office of the White Star Line was told that the Titanic was in trouble, the line's vice president, Philip Franklin announced: "We place absolute confidence in the Titanic. We believe the boat is unsinkable." He had no way of knowing that while he was uttering those very words, the Titanic was already either on the bottom of the ocean or on its way there. What made people so confident that the ship couldn't sink? Perhaps it was the ship's watertight compartments. Or maybe it was the fact that so many scientific advancements were taking place in the beginning of the twentieth century that people had absolute faith in science and technology.

If there was a bright spot connected to the tragedy of the Titanic sinking, it was that the disaster spawned the first International Safety of Life at Sea Convention. This convention led to today's International Maritime Organization, which governs safety at sea across the world.

Subsequent chapters of this book will cover specific ways we can protect ourselves from future economic disasters that lie in wait for the unsuspecting investor as surely as those icebergs lay in wait for the Titanic. We will explore lessons we learned, or should have learned, on how to invest sensibly and ensure ourselves a secure and carefree retirement. When it comes to retirement planning, just like the iceberg that sunk the Titanic, it's not always what you see directly in front of you, but the dangers that may lurk beneath the surface that can sink your financial ship.

Chapter Two

No Fumbling in the Red Zone

"When you ain't got nothing,' You got nothin' to lose."
~ Bob Dylan, Like A Rolling Stone

    In football, the "red zone" is the area between the 20-yard line and the goal line. It's the last piece of property you must fight over before you score a touchdown. They seem to be the hardest yards to get, too. For one thing, the field is compressed. Receivers can't go "long" because the field is too short for that now. Like a cornered animal, the defensive team has its back against the wall and can be counted upon to take the ball away any way they can. Offensive players say the defensive line is stiffer, giving ground more grudgingly the closer to you get to the goal line. Ball carriers claim the tackles are harder, more jarring in the "red zone." Defensive players are not trying just to knock you down; they want to knock the ball loose. Coaches even tell their defensive players to "tackle the ball" in the "red zone."
    Offensive coaches usually call more conservative plays in the "red zone." Unless they have a talented passer with a keen eye and an accurate arm, coaches are usually content to grind it out on the line of scrimmage rather than trust the forward pass. They know that there is always the field goal if they fail to make a first down. Runners are told to hold the ball with both hands when they run and, whatever you do, **don't fumble!**
    Many a close game has come down to the wire with one team a few points away from a win, only to see the game slip away due to a heartbreaking fumble in those last few yards.

Finding Safe Harbor in Retirement

The analogy to saving for retirement is clearly this: You have worked too hard and too long, and saved too arduously to risk losing it all in the "red zone" of retirement, which is a good way to characterize the final 10 years of your working life. As was documented by the previous chapter, the most obvious hazards to a worry-free retirement is inordinate market risk.

Some struggle with this, but it's really quite simple. First of all, there is no truth to the adage: "No Risk – No Reward." There are plenty of ways nowadays to obtain better than average and quite respectable growth on your money without taking inordinate risk. Second, how do you characterize inordinate risk? Risk tolerance is one way. How much risk can you personally stand?

When I meet with prospective clients in my office in Mooresville, North Carolina, I make it a point to listen much more than I talk, especially during my first meeting. I have to know certain things about their financial lives that only they can tell me if I am to determine whether we are a good fit to work together. During one such interview, a gentleman told me where he drew the line on risk – if it started interfering with his sleep.

"I just don't want to wake up in the middle of the night, worried about my investments," he said, adding with a smile that he needed his "beauty sleep." Then he grew serious and told me of how the big market correction of 2000 taught him a valuable lesson. He had stayed up many nights during that market meltdown wondering what to do. Should he cut his losses and get out "while the getting was good?" But what would happen if the market started back up and he wasn't there to capitalize on the bounce back? But what if there was no bounce back? What if this was a deep black hole from which there was no return? What then?

I thought about that a lot. It makes sense, doesn't it? If your investments in the stock market interfere with your getting a good night's rest, then it may be that you need to think about what you are doing and why you are doing it?

It All Depends

There's how much *could* you stand if your portfolio is getting pummeled by a market downturn, and there's how much *should* you stand. As they say about life in general, and it is also true in this matter of risk: "Different strokes for different folks." How much risk you *should* take on will depend on factors including age, income, current savings and general investment knowledge. Risk tolerance is a measure of your willingness to accept higher risk or volatility in exchange for higher potential returns. Those with high tolerance are aggressive investors, willing to accept losing their capital in search for higher returns. Those with a low tolerance, also called risk averse, are conservative investors who are more concerned with capital preservation. Neither one is ideal.

For example, consider two people with exactly same age, same wage and same job with same career options for the future. However, one is an aggressive investor who likes to bet on anything he can get his hands on, while the other is a conservative investor who keeps her earnings and spends frugally. Despite having identical financial circumstances, they have very different risk tolerances and probably dramatically different portfolios.

Also consider one's financial capacity to tolerate risk. Consider how three investors would be affected by a 50 percent drop in the values of their portfolios.

JIM is 76 years old and has made billions as a leader of industry. His estimated net worth is $1 billion.

SUSAN is in her late 40s and has a family to support. She is slowly nearing retirement age and is worth around $2 million.

SAM is 30 years old, is just beginning his investment career with a current net worth of around $100,000.

BOB AND WANDA are 63 years old respectively, own a small grocery store and an adjoining coin-operated car wash. They have worked hard and saved diligently and have managed to accumulate $500,000, nearly all of which they have invested in mutual funds.

What would a loss of 50 percent do to **Jim's** net worth? He would be down to $500 million. Would he be happy about that loss? Of course not! Would he survive it? Of course he would. So would **Susan**. She would have the capacity to absorb a financial hit of 50 percent. She has many more years to save and invest before she has to think about retirement and she is still "sitting on a cool million."

A loss of 50 percent for **Sam** would be quite a setback, but, then again, he has his entire investing life ahead of him. If the past is any indication of the future, the market will *eventually* recover and he will be made whole and have many more years to invest.

But what about **Bob** and **Wanda**? They are in the worst shape of all. They are not suffering, but they aren't mega-wealthy either. They do not have time to ride out the ebbs of the market, waiting for the surge of the flow to take them back to the top of the wave pattern. The timing – losing such a significant portion of their savings this close to retirement – could not have been worse. They will likely have to postpone retirement and continue working until they can regroup financially.

Rules of Thumb

A rule of thumb is a principle with a broad application, not to be taken as an absolute or a specific. The term is thought to originate with wood workers who used the width of their thumbs, which when depressed on a flat surface is more or less an inch, for measuring things. Imprecise, maybe, butan easy and convenient standard. When it comes to risk tolerance, some rule of thumb are:

- The younger you are, the more risk you should be willing to tolerate. You have a longer time horizon in which to grow assets.
- The shorter your investment time horizon, the less money you should invest in the stock market. Naturally, retired individuals and those approaching retirement will have a shorter time horizon than those still working.
- Your goals should determine how you invest. If your goal is aggressive growth, you should be willing to take on more risk. If your goal is preservation of assets and guaranteed income, then the opposite will be true.
- Your income is an important consideration. Do you feel your income will decline? Then you should be more risk averse. Will it increase dramatically? Then your tolerance for risk should be higher.
- Do you have an emergency fund set aside? I'm talking about liquid money in a checking or savings account, CDs or money market funds. Money you can put your hands on to cover an unexpected expense without dipping into your savings. Before you consider placing assets at risk for investment purposes, you should have at least six months income set aside as an emergency fund.

- How much investment experience do you have. The more experience, then the higher your risk tolerance should be and vice versa.
- ***Follow the Rule of 100.*** Take your age and subtract it from 100. That is the acceptable percentage of your money to have at risk. Another way to do it is to put a percent sign after it, and as a ***rule of thumb*** that is the percentage of your assets that should be kept completely safe from market risk.

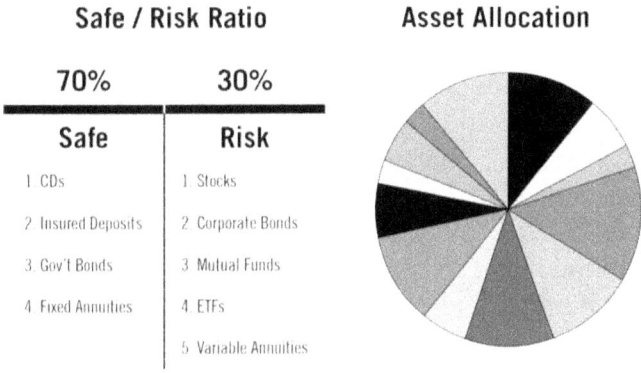

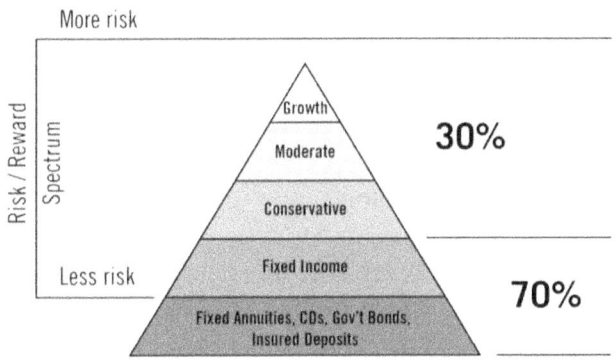

Keep in mind that the Rule of 100 works both ways. Young people put enough of their money at risk in the stock market. If someone is age 25, then 75 percent of their assets should be invested and the rest should be available for emergencies. On the other hand, if someone is 75 years of age the reverse is true. From where I watch the financial world, I believe following the Rule of 100 would benefit all age categories in both the long and the short run.

The Three Phases of Our Financial Lives

The three phases of our financial lives are:

- Accumulation (Ages 20-50)
- Preservation (Ages 50-65)
- Distribution (Ages 65+)

The accumulation phase is for the young (er) folks, mainly. It's the working years. I like to refer to these years as the years when you are in "paycheck mode." You grow up, you go to school, you get married (or not), you have a family (or not), and you get a job. Hopefully you are a diligent saver and you sink at least 10-15 percent of your salary each pay period into a retirement savings/investment account of some type and let it grow. These days, with pensions going the way of the Dodo bird, the savings vehicle will likely be a 401(k), 403(b), or some other tax-deferred retirement savings plan. Some who are in the accumulation phase of life are entrepreneurs, perhaps owners of a small business. If that is your situation, then you should have your own retirement savings plan, perhaps using an IRA (Individual Retirement Account), a Keogh plan, Roth IRA, cash value life insurance plan, etc.

During the accumulation phase of your financial life, the one thing you have on your side is time. The way to make it work for you is by steadily investing money in your retirement account and letting it grow until you retire. The key here is to be regular and consistent with your contributions and to leave it alone and let it grow. One of the functions of the emergency fund is to enable you to resist the temptation of dipping into your savings when emergencies arise. You know how it is. You have good intentions of putting the money back into the piggy bank but life goes on, you forget, and the interest on that money is lost forever.

If you are employed, and your employer offers to match a portion of what you contribute to your savings plan, by all means take advantage of that. It's free money! I see far too many young people opt for new toys and whatever else money will buy instead of taking full advantage of their tax deferred savings plans.

Dollar Cost Averaging

When you are in your younger working years, if you are consistent with your savings, you can benefit from something called "dollar cost averaging." Here's how it works. Let's say that you have a job with a 401(k). Your employer has made an agreement with you that for every dollar you set aside into the program, the company will match it up to 6 percent of your paycheck. Again, that's ***free money.*** Please take advantage of this by contributing the maximum allowed by law into your 401(k). In 2013 the maximum you could contribute to a 401(k) program was $17,500 per year. If you're age 50 or over there is a makeup provision that allows you to put in up to $23,000 per year. At the very least, put enough money into the plan to get the employer match. It's pretty stupid to turn down free money!! It's a win-win situation, both for you and your employer. The company gets a tax deduction for its share of the contribution (and you thought they were just that generous!), and you get to defer taxes on your portion. The money you contribute to a 401(k) usually goes into an investment account where a custodian uses the funds to buy shares of mutual funds. The stock market can be a dangerous place if you are a one-time investor with limited experience or if you are approaching retirement and put all your eggs in that very risky basket. But when you are in your accumulation years, the volatility of the stock market actually works to your advantage. Here's what I mean: Your regular contribution goes into your 401(k) each week and is used to buy as many shares of XYZ mutual fund as that amount of money can buy. If XYZ mutual fund shares *increase* in value, that's great! Your account value just went up. If XYZ mutual fund shares *decrease* in value, that's great too! Your contribution just bought more shares. Those XYZ shares will fatten up some day, and because time is on your side, you can afford to wait. This is not the case with older folks.

Preservation Phase

The Preservation phase of our financial life cycle is when we begin to think in terms of protecting what we have accumulated. My grandfather was not a financial professional, but he was a man with an abundance of common sense. One of his favorite expressions when it came to money and savings was: "It's not what you make, it's what you keep."

The bigger our nest egg, the more naturally inclined we are to guard and protect it. Having assets at our disposal usually impels us to make them as productive as possible. When we are in our 20s, 30s and 40s, and are accumulating our savings, we usually attach a purpose to that savings program. Perhaps our maternal and paternal instincts are involved. We are saving that money so that after we are gone, our family, our children, and perhaps even our children's children will be cared for. Maybe we envision their world to be a bit more difficult than ours. Perhaps we want to spare them some of the bumps in the road we encountered. Or maybe we saved and invested with the idea in mind that one of these days, when our hair turned gray, but we were still active enough to enjoy it, we would travel. Perhaps to visit relatives living in far away states…or even countries. Or maybe just to see the sights. I know of one couple who have a bumper sticker on the back of their motor home that reads: *"We Are Spending our Children's Inheritance."* And they are pretty darn serious about it. They have stickers for every state they have been to in that behemoth, and they have just about covered the 48!

Regardless of your purpose, it would be a shame to work and save for all those years and then, because of some sudden change in the economic climate, lose half of it because you had too much of it at risk in the stock market. If you have accumulated some money, you are also walking around with a target on your back for investment schemes, scams that prey on senior citizens, or those who will sue you at the drop of a hat if they think you have some material wealth.

The preservation mode, for the most part, is when you are still working, but you are approaching retirement age. You are still contributing to your savings, but you are no longer protected by "dollar cost averaging" because of the time factor. In fact, once you retire, instead of being protected by "dollar cost averaging," you can be the victim of *"**reverse** dollar cost averaging."* Here's how that works:

Let's say that you are in full retirement. When you stopped working, you also stopped contributing to that tax-deferred 401(k) retirement plan, too. Now the money river starts to flow the other way. Instead of contributing to that fund, you must now draw from it. Those withdrawals are made with the same regularity as your earlier deposits were made, only the withdrawals are much more, since they must replace what your entire paycheck would have been had you still be working.

Those paychecks you are withdrawing are produced by **selling** shares of stock in those same mutual funds. If the price of the shares fluctuate, which they always do, you still write yourself the same paycheck from your retirement account. So if the share prices go up, you sell fewer shares. If the share prices go down, you sell more shares. Either way, you are withdrawing the same amount. If a market crash occurs, and the value of your account goes down dramatically, those losses will be real and earnest and since you are no longer contributing to the account, you are no longer buying shares on the cheap to replace those losses. Also, factor in that you are depleting the account at a faster rate and that every share you sell is one less share that will be working for you in the account.

This is one of the reasons why, as a financial advisor with a conscience and sensitivity to those approaching retirement, I advocate safe money investing once you have the retirement finish line in sight, and insist on safe-money investing once you cross it. I have seen too many individuals lose money they couldn't afford to lose because of a stock market reversal, and then have no way of recovering those losses. In subsequent chapters, we will provide suggestions on how to avoid the trap of "reverse dollar cost averaging" by following some simple strategies that remove the possibility of loss.

Finding Safe Harbor in Retirement

ORDER OF RETURNS

John

Age	Hypothetical stock market gains or losses	Withdrawl at start of year	Nest Egg at start of year
64			$500,000
65	-10.14%	$25,000	$500,000
66	-13.04%	$25,750	$426,839
67	-23.37%	$26,523	$348,776
68	14.62%	$27,318	$246,956
69	2.03%	$28,138	$251,750
70	12.40%	$28,982	$228,146
71	27.25%	$29,851	$223,862
72	-6.56%	$30,747	$246,879
73	26.31%	$31,669	$201,956
74	4.46%	$32,619	$215,084
75	7.06%	$33,958	$190,610
76	-1.54%	$34,606	$168,090
77	34.11%	$35,644	$131,429
78	20.26%	$36,713	$128,458
79	31.01%	$37,815	$110,335
80	26.67%	$38,949	$95,008
81	19.53%	$40,118	$71,009
82	26.38%	$36,923	$36,923
83	-38.49%	$0	$0
84	3.00%		
85	13.62%		
86	3.53%		
87	26.38%		
88	23.45%		
89	12.78%		

Average Return: 8.03%
Total withdrawal: $580,963

Susan

Age	Hypothetical stock market gains or losses	Withdrawl at start of year	Nest Egg at start of year
64			$500,000
65	12.78%	$25,000	$500,000
66	23.45%	$25,750	$535,716
67	26.38%	$26,523	$629,575
68	3.53%	$27,318	$762,140
69	13.62%	$28,138	$760,755
70	3.00%	$28,982	$832,396
71	-38.49%	$29,851	$827,524
72	26.38%	$30,747	$490,684
73	19.53%	$31,669	$581,270
74	26.67%	$32,619	$656,916
75	31.01%	$33,598	$790,788
76	20.26%	$34,606	$991,981
77	34.11%	$35,644	$1,151,375
78	-1.54%	$36,713	$1,496,314
79	7.06%	$37,815	$1,437,133
80	4.46%	$38,949	$1,498,042
81	26.31%	$40,118	$1,524,231
82	-6.56%	$41,321	$1,874,535
83	27.25%	$42,561	$1,712,970
84	12.40%	$43,838	$2,125,604
85	2.03%	$45,153	$2,339,923
86	14.62%	$46,507	$2,341,297
87	-23.37%	$47,903	$2,630,297
88	-13.04%	$49,340	$1,978,993
89	-10.14%	$50,820	$1,677,975

Average Return: 8.03%
Total withdrawal: $911,482

Order of Returns

There is one thing retirees need to be very concerned about, especially when planning for lifetime income. I call it the "order of returns," or "sequence of returns." I'm sure you have heard the Wall Street myth that if you're in the market for the long haul, you'll earn 8 to 10 percent on your money (you can decide for yourself what the "long haul" is at age 65 or 75). That 8 -10 percent deal is not always true, but let's give them the benefit of the doubt. As the illustration above demonstrates, both portfolios earned an annualized rate of return of 8.03 percent over a 25 year period. But, because of the timing (order of returns) John is broke at age 83, while Susan is just fine. So here's my point: Do you want to take the chance that you'll end up like John? In my opinion, it's simply not wise, especially when products and strategies exist today that can eliminate this worry.

As discussed in a previous chapter, older people fear running out of money in their sunset years more than they fear snakes, spiders and even death. That's understandable, too. We all shudder at the thought of becoming a burden on our loved ones.

If you are in the distribution/income phase of your financial life, and your assets are invested in the stock market and the market nosedives suddenly, your losses are compounded because of the timing involved. Fifty-three percent of those surveyed by the Allianz poll said they saw their net worth drop significantly during the economic downturn of 2008. That is only a statistic until you get to know some of the people who were hurt by that economic catastrophe. Shortly after the 2008 crash, one couple who attended a seminar at which I spoke on income planning were almost in tears. They told me that before the crash they had a little over $200,000 in their nest egg. They had figured that, if they were careful, they could make the transition from self-employed business owners to retirement without much change in lifestyle. They were counting on their Social Security, the proceeds from the sale of their jointly owned flower shop, and their $200,000 retirement savings to see them through. They had their retirement budget figured down to the penny. They had trusted their broker explicitly, expecting that he protect their investments from loss.

They said they were shocked and dismayed at how they had lost 40 percent of their account virtually overnight.

They were forced to put their retirement plans on hold. Originally, they had planned to sell the flower shop to a nephew who had helped them run the business. With the small consulting fee they would receive as part of the buyout, they had intended to travel. They had wanted to spend some time with their daughter and her husband, and their two grandsons, ages 8 and 10. They were looking forward to taking the boys to Walt Disney World and touring the Everglades. They had been a few months away from accomplishing that dream when the bottom fell out. It wasn't just the irreplaceable 40 percent of their savings that was gone. The calm and secure feeling they once had about the future was gone too. They had resigned themselves that they would have to continue running their business for another five years. They took steps to move what remained of their nest egg into a guaranteed investment account. They also said they planned to cut back on entertaining and dining out to bolster their retirement fund.

I share these details with you to make a point. Statistics are one thing. But the human cost of risky investing is translated from numbers to shattered hopes and dreams. This couple is typical of many others with whom I have come in contact since I began my practice. Many of them were angry. From their point of view, they had trusted professionals who had bitterly disappointed them.

"Why didn't anyone tell us this was coming," the woman asked.

The truth is, no one knows when a market crash will occur. If they did, they would certainly have a moral obligation to warn as many as possible to seek economic shelter. But their broker had no way of knowing. And to be fair, their broker may not have been able to offer any solution except move them to a cash position had he possessed advance knowledge of the Wall Street collapse.

I believe that financial advisors should be as responsible for the wealth of their clients as doctors are for the health of their patients. When it comes to your health, you are the one who bears the ultimate responsibility. You are the only one that can make sure that you maintain a proper diet and get enough exercise. No one can avoid unhealthy lifestyle habits but you. Similarly, you are the one who is ultimately responsible for your portfolio. It is up to you to know your risk tolerance and communicate that to your financial handlers. It is your responsibility to pay attention to your risk meter and recognize it when your assets are in danger. But you expect your doctor to be well informed enough to spot it when something is wrong. You expect your personal physician to be so well acquainted with your medical history and your physical condition that he or she can advise you how to avoid a heart attack or stroke. They bear an awesome responsibility in that regard and, for the most part, they have earned our trust in that regard. Likewise, you expect a financial professional to be accountable if, through bad advice or simply no advice at all, you lose a significant amount of money under his or her guidance.

The bottom line is this. Stock market risk is probably acceptable when you are young, for reasons described above. But not when you're older and nearing retirement. That's when it's time to rein in the risk and look for safe-money alternatives.

To continue the medical metaphor, I don't know of very many people who, after they reach adulthood, still go to a pediatrician for a physical examination. That doesn't mean that your pediatrician isn't a skilled physician. No doubt he or she is quite good at treating children. But your body is different at age 30 than it is at age 10 (not to mention the difference between age 30 and age 60!) Physiologically, you are a different person. You are taller with more muscle mass. By the time you reach adulthood, your medical needs are completely different. The medicines used to treat the ailments of a child will differ in both dosage and chemical makeup from those used to treat an adult. It is the same with your wealth. Why not see a specialist who knows what to look for and one who knows how to help mend whatever may need mending. When a person is in his or her 60s and ready to make that transition from worker to retired person, and they seek financial advice, a lot more is riding on that advice now. The preservation/distribution phase is more complex than the accumulation phase. Taxes are different. Income needs are drawn along more critical lines. Contingencies, such as a health crisis, weren't as prominent in your 20s and 30s, and they must be accounted for. Retirement planning is highly specialized and there is no cookie-cutter approach to it… none that work, anyway. Retirement plans are as individual as fingerprints. No two are alike, because no individual financial situation is identical. Not only are the rules different for taxes, your perspective on things such as risk tolerance, safety of principle, growth and liquidity are different in the distribution phase. Ignoring these differences can lead to financial heartache.

Time to Make Good Decisions

You never want to fumble the ball when you are playing football. But for some reason, fumbling the ball in midfield is not as devastating to the morale of the team as fumbling on the five-yard line. The reason is simple. You worked so hard to get to the goal line. You were almost there. And because of a mistake in execution or perhaps a risky play call, you lost all that ground you had gained and now you're back on defense. Financially speaking, it's not just loss of morale that is at stake – it's the loss of perhaps thousands of dollars and losing out on a worry-free retirement and the independence those assets could have meant. That's why proper planning is more important than ever when you are in the "red zone" of retirement.

Number four on USA TODAY's 10 hardest things to do in sports is hitting a golf ball straight and long. It's mainly because of the physics involved. The collision of the club head with the ball lasts less than 1/1,000th of a second, but in that tiny time span a lot takes place. A tiny miscalculation during the swing will cause the ball to be off target by several yards when it lands.

If an airplane takes off from an airport at the equator, intending to circumnavigate the globe but is off course by just one degree, by the time it returns to the same longitude it will be approximately 500 miles off course.

When you are planning for your retirement, it is important to make good, sound investing decisions. Actions you take and plans you make now with your finances will be relatively small strokes in comparison with the dramatic positive effects they will have years in to the future. The reverse is true. Actions **untaken** and decisions **unmade** will have dramatic **negative** effects on you financially in the future. Financial planning is much different as you approach retirement than it is when you are in the accumulation years. If your decisions are off the mark in your younger years, the cost will be exponentially greater in your retirement years. And most planning errors are avoidable as the next chapter makes clear.

Chapter Three

Common *Myth*-stakes Retirees Make

    Let's face it. We all make mistakes. Growing up, I was always taught that making mistakes is simply part of the learning process. I suppose that is true, because I have certainly learned from my mistakes over the years. But when it comes to handling your money, the closer you get to retirement, the more costly your mistakes can be. There was a time in America when retired folks just set the income dial to "auto pilot" and waited for their pension checks roll in. Not anymore. Nowadays most retirees are responsible for handling their *own* savings and producing their *own* incomes. It is no time for miscalculations.

    One of the reasons I devote a significant portion of my time to conducting public seminars is because I believe education about money misconceptions is important. Outdated ideas about wealth management and antiquated investment doctrines have cost American retirees much more money than the scams and frauds that capture the headlines. Bernie Madoff pulled off the biggest Ponzi scheme in history. And how much did he end up stealing from those he defrauded? Something like $65 billion? How much money did retirement accounts lose in the stock market crash of 2008? According to figures released that year by the Congressional Budget Office, more than $2 trillion! That's *trillion* with a "T." How much of that lost wealth could have been preserved by education on safe investing for retirees and those approaching retirement?

    My grandfather was a Wisconsin dairy farmer. He taught me many things during the summers I spent there. For one thing, he believed in hard work and would not tolerate a slacker. Looking back, I think that

I never worked harder than I did as a teenager on that dairy farm. At the time, of course, I didn't realize the value of all of the life lessons I learned there, but later on in life they would serve me well. My grandfather was painfully honest. His word was his bond and he would keep any promise he made even if it hurt. He often did business involving thousands of dollars on a handshake. He was fond of saying, "What's right is right – regardless of what anybody says." It took me years to fully understand the depth of that simple adage. He was referring to what is both morally right, and what is practically right as well. In a moral sense, there is a right way to live your life – following the golden rule, for example: "Do unto others as you would have them do unto you." In a practical sense, there is just a right way to do certain things. Take planting corn, for example. Plant when it's too wet and the crop will grow unevenly and won't fare well when the soil turns dry during the summer. Plant corn when it is too dry and you run the risk of the seed not germinating on time. As Grandpa would say, "There's just a right way and a wrong way to do things, and what's right is right."

What's right is right when it comes to investing and wealth management, too. In my professional life I have always felt an obligation to point people in the right direction in this regard. I still find great satisfaction in debunking investing myths.

Myth - Mutual Funds Are Always Great Investments

Take, for example, the myths associated with mutual funds. Most people believe that mutual funds are a great place to put money, and *sometimes* they are. Let me give it to you straight – They are great places to put your money - just *not all the time!*

I like what David F. Swensen said in his eye-opening book *Unconventional Success*: "Overwhelmingly, mutual funds extract enormous sums from investors in exchange for providing a shocking disservice."

Swensen, who is chief investment officer at Yale University, wrote an opinion piece that appeared in the New York Times August 13, 2011, in which he said: "For decades, the mutual fund industry, which manages more than $13 trillion for 90 million Americans, has employed market volatility to produce profits for itself far more reliably than it has produced returns for its investors. Too often, investors believe that mutual funds provide a safe haven, placing a misguided trust in brokers, advisers and fund managers. In fact, the industry has a history of delivering inferior results to investors, and its regulators do not provide effective oversight."

Right on, Mr. Swensen! But guess where most of the money Americans are socking away for retirement sits. You guessed it – mutual funds! They are still the number one vehicle Americans use for retirement planning. Think about it. Workaday Bob and workaday Sue put aside money each week from their paycheck into a 401(k), 403(b), or some other retirement savings plan. Where does that money go? Mutual funds. When you work for a large company that sponsors a 401(k), for example, you will usually have a counselor from the personnel office sit down with you and review your options. You are usually given a menu of investments to choose from and typically these investment options take the form of either stock mutual funds or bond mutual funds. These funds are usually held by one of two companies – Fidelity or Vanguard. These mutual fund families hold 80 percent of all retirement plan money in the United States. Can these investments lose money? Of course they can! Just ask any who saw significant portions of their fortunes evaporate in the last market crash.

As the employees get older and approach retirement age, advisors representing these fund families will sometimes tell them to reduce their risk by placing more of their assets in bond mutual funds and less in stock mutual funds. But here's the problem – going from one set of mutual funds to another set of mutual funds is a bit like having your car repainted to improve its performance. The truth is, all mutual funds have risk and are costly in terms of fees and expenses. When interest rates are low, bond funds are more risky than stock funds.

But wait a minute! Don't reputable analysts look at these funds and give them ratings according to their performances? Can we not rely on those ratings to make sure that we pick winners and not losers? You would come to that conclusion if you were to listen to the mutual fund companies, brokers and the financial advisors who aggressively market mutual funds. The funds you will hear the most about are the ones which are rated four-star and five-star funds by Morningstar, the Chicago-based arbiter of investment performance. But all that rating system does is identify the few funds that performed well in the past year. It provides no help in finding next year's winners. The losers that used to be winners are never advertised. In fact, they limp off to mutual fund burial grounds never to be heard from again. It is a sleight-of-hand maneuver used to make gullible investors imagine that it is possible to time the market. Markets, by their very nature, are unpredictable – the stock market in particular is volatile and given to sudden, unexpected changes.

Two myths of my childhood, perpetuated by a well-meaning mother, were that touching a toad would give you warts and that if you swallowed your chewing gum, it would take seven years to digest. She meant well. To this day I won't touch a toad, and still don't chew gum (just kidding)! The point is that if you're told something often enough, you start to believe it whether it's true or not. Companies that manage mutual funds perpetuate the myth that certain fund managers are imbued with a special gift for seeing into the future and predicting which way the market will go. The fact is, companies that manage for-profit mutual funds have a conflict of interest between (a) producing profits for their owners, and (b) generating profits for mutual fund investors. If you run the numbers, the management companies have made out pretty well over the last few decades while investors have suffered below-market returns. Why? Often because of the useless churning of investments within the investor's mutual fund portfolio. Fund managers often buy and sell within the funds to increase their compensation. That's right – fund managers make money on each trade they make through the broker/dealer regardless of how the investment performs.

Swensen points out that in 2010, investors redeemed $152 billion from one-star, two-star and three-star funds and placed $304 billion in four-star and five-star funds. According to Swensen, this goes on year in and year out. The churning of investor portfolios benefits only the churners, not the mutual fund owners. Actually, since the mutual fund industry uses the star-rating system to encourage performance-chasing (selling funds that performed poorly and buying funds that performed well), investors end up actually buying low and selling high – which is exactly the opposite of the formula for trading success!

As to the overall performance of mutual funds, would it surprise you to know that according to some researchers, from 1984-1998, only eight of 203 mutual funds that exceeded $100 million in assets actually beat the Vanguard 500 index? That is a 4 percent chance of success! Or as one columnist put it: "Your odds, then, of picking a "winning" mutual fund during that time were less than 4 percent By way of comparison, if you get dealt two face cards in blackjack, and your inner idiot shouts, "Hit me!", you have about an 8 percent chance of winning."

According to Swensen, the ill-advised buying and selling of funds continues to cost the investing public a substantial sum year after year mainly because investors naïvely trust their brokers and advisers. Two business school professors from Arizona State University, Jay Koehler and Molly Mercer, conducted studies on investors and documented their wiliness to believe what the hype of the mutual fund companies when they advertise certain funds as winners. Koehler and Mercer call it "cherry picked data." When a mutual fund company advertises a 31 percent return on one fund, investors gather around like moths to a light bulb and their interest spreads to other mutual funds offered by the same company, even if they have average or below average returns. What no one bothers to tell them is that the 31 percent return is an anomaly. Also not advertised are the fees charged within mutual funds, which can range anywhere from 1 to 6 percent. Costs are the biggest problem with mutual funds. These costs eat into your return, and they are the main reason why the majority of funds end up with sub-par performance.

What's even more disturbing is the way the fund industry hides costs through layers of financial complexity and jargon. Some critics of the industry say that mutual fund companies get away with the fees they charge only because average investors simply do not understand what they are paying for.

Myth – Social Security Will Take Care of Me

Let me just rip off the bandage quickly on this one. No. It won't. Not unless you are prepared to live below the poverty level. The more you earn during your working years, the more you contribute into the Social Security trust fund, and therefore the more your retirement benefits will be. Those who contribute the maximum into the program will get the maximum out of the program.

As I was compiling research for this book, I learned that in 2013, almost 58 million Americans would receive $816 billion in Social Security benefits and that the average individual monthly payout was $1,262. For a single person age 65 or older that's not much above the poverty level, which, as of 2012, was $10,788 annual income.

Ironically, if you earned enough to contribute the maximum into the system, chances are you will not be happy with the lifestyle that even the maximum Social Security check will be able to provide. Even if you paid in the maximum, and even if you waited until you reach age 70 to start your benefits, the maximum you would receive (as of 2013) was $3,350 per month. Can you live on that? In the face of rising costs, higher taxes and just general, run-of-the-mill unforeseen expenses, you have to ask yourself, in the immortal words of Clint Eastwood in one of those *Dirty Harry* movies he made so popular in the 1970s, "Do you feel lucky?"

As mentioned in chapter one of this book, these stark facts still don't prevent a significant number of Americans (64 percent according to one survey) from viewing Social Security as the main source of income in retirement. Experts say you should not plan on Social Security for more than 30 percent of your annual income. It's a nice supplement, a nice safety net, but not a foundation pillar of retirement planning. Social Security should be viewed as a part of an overall retirement income plan if at all possible.

Myth – Social Security Won't Even Be Here for Me

If you are a baby boomer (born between 1946 and 1964), relax. You'll get your money. If you are in your 30s and 40s, however, (hand waggle) there is no guarantee.

In doing research for this book, I discovered that life expectancy in the 1930s for men was 60 years of age and 64 for women. When the Social Security Act was passed by Congress in 1935, the retirement age was set at 65 (now you can take early Social Security at age 62). That means that the lawmakers and President Franklin D. Roosevelt probably never intended for the program to pay out much in the way of retirement benefits. They had no way of knowing that 21st Century Americans would be living well into their 90s. That is precisely why some changes will have to be made if the system is to be preserved for the generations that come after the baby boomers. Trustees of the system predict that, unless something is done, the Social Security trust fund will only be able to fund 75 percent of benefits by 2033. Proposed reforms include raising the retirement age, raising payroll taxes and perhaps even revising the benefit formula in one way or another. What reforms are made will take place over a number of years and today's seniors won't feel it. As of 2013, there were 2.8 workers for each Social Security beneficiary. According to the Social Security Administration, by 2033, there will be 2.1 workers for each beneficiary. By 2033, the number of older Americans will increase from 45.1 million today to 77.4 million. Will Social Security be here in its present form for future generations? At this point, that is anybody's guess.

Myth – Risk Equals Reward

Risk equals reward? Who told you that one? Some financial professionals will try to tell you that the only way to grow your money is to play the Wall Street version of the great roulette wheel. "No Risk – No Reward," is the mantra of those whose only approach to wealth management is through equities and equities only. I will agree that the more risk you take with your assets the more reward you are *exposed* to, and therefore the more reward it is *possible* to acquire. But that doesn't mean that risk *equals* reward.

A theme you will see recurring throughout this book is that age plays a very important role in how much risk you should take. In chapter two of this book, you were introduced to the "Rule of 100." Take your age and put a percent sign after it and that represents the amount of your wealth you should keep absolutely safe and out of risk's way. But, aside from an emergency fund, I enthusiastically encourage you to place the rest of your assets in sensible investments that involve some risk, including equities. This is where you need the guidance of a Registered Investment Advisor who has a fiduciary responsibility to help you avoid overdoing either side of the equation. I highly encourage you to find an advisor that's skilled with insurance planning, as well as with equity planning. Insurance companies can provide a huge benefit when planning for retirement, but they are often overlooked by our friends on Wall Street. Please don't make that mistake!

Myth – Rely on the 4 Percent Rule

This is one of those myths that persist because it used to be true. There was a time when the "4 percent rule" was a staple of financial advisors. If you've never heard of it, it goes something like this: Say you retired with $1 million. Using the 4 percent rule, you could withdraw $40,000 (4 percent of $1 million) for the remainder of your life and even adjust it upward for inflation, and not run out of money for 20 or so years after retirement. The 4 percent rule called for rebalancing the retirement account in a 60-40 percent mix of stocks and bonds throughout one's retirement.

The idea for this strategy got its start in 1998 when three professors at Trinity University, San Antonio, Texas, kept working with three factors – life expectancies, withdrawal rates and historical returns of the stock market – until they came up with a formula. Once they plugged in the life expectancy data and the market returns data, they played with different withdrawal rates trying to get as close as possible to the 100 percent success factor of not running out of money. Four percent turned out to be the magic number.

When they released their findings, it suddenly became the immutable gospel of investing for brokers and financial advisors who preferred solely market-based solutions.

The problem with the 4 percent rule, however, is that the data fed into the calculations was gathered from market returns of the 1980s and 1990s when the market knew only one direction – up. Unless you have been asleep under a rock for the decade or so, I don't have to tell you that times have changed a bit since then. That, plus most people don't have a million-dollar nest egg to play with.

With market volatility becoming a constant feature of the economic landscape and life expectancy on the rise, the 4 percent rule is about as obsolete as cassette tape players and film cameras. Used to work. Doesn't now. End of story.

Note: These past few years various studies have come out disputing the 4 percent rule. T.Rowe Price, The Putnam Institute, AARP, The Wharton School of Business, and the Government Accountability Office (GAO) to name a few. A quick "Google Search" will find them.

Chapter Four

The Three Money Worlds

When I was 12 years old, I had a paper route delivering the daily edition of the Milwaukee Journal Sentinel. If your mind conjures up the image of a boy on a bicycle pedaling down a tree-lined street, tossing rolled up newspapers onto lawns and porches in the late afternoon sun, you're pretty close. On the day I collected for the week's delivery, I worked harder and longer than the other days. But it was also my favorite day of the week because it was my payday. After I reimbursed the newspaper company for the papers I had delivered, I got to keep what was left over.

My first stop, after I had finished collecting from my customers, was the local IGA store where I would part with some of the proceeds to buy candy. Each IGA store (the acronym stands for Independent Grocers Alliance) was individually owned, and quite often, family-operated. I can never forget our local neighborhood IGA store because of a wooden sign that hung right above the store's front door. Etched in block letters were these words: **"Low Prices, High Quality, Great Service –** *Pick any two.***"**

Even at the tender age of 12 I knew what that meant. Many things in life are about tradeoffs. Take the candy for example. I could either have the money in my pocket or the candy in my hand, but I couldn't have both. There was a trade off involved. At age 12, I opted for the candy. For the store manager, the sign was merely a clever way of letting his customers know that they could, for example, expect low prices and high quality, but they would have to sacrifice service. In those days, bag boys took your groceries out to the parking lot and put them in your car for you.

Finding Safe Harbor in Retirement

Why do people shop at Nordstrom's? They want high quality and great service but they don't expect it to be cheap. In the world of investing, there are three things that are involved in the tradeoff

- High growth potential
- Complete safety of principle ----- **PICK ANY TWO!!**
- Absolute liquidity

THREE MONEY WORLDS

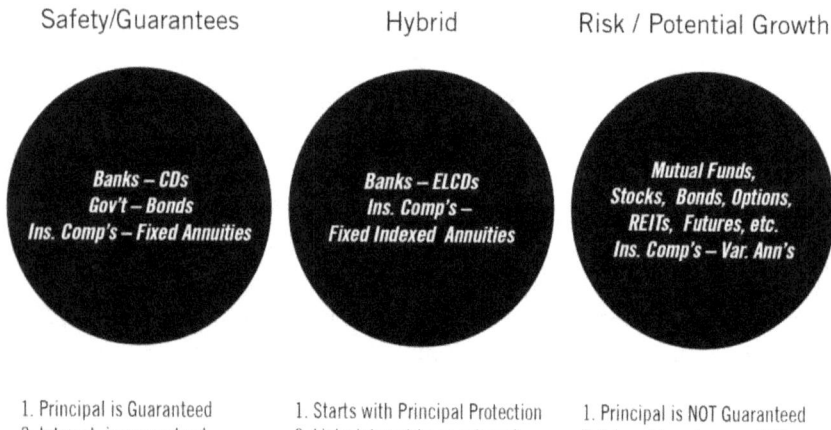

GUARANTEED PRODUCTS   **INVESTMENTS**

Safety/Guarantees   Hybrid   Risk / Potential Growth

Banks – CDs   Banks – ELCDs   Mutual Funds,
Gov't – Bonds   Ins. Comp's –   Stocks, Bonds, Options,
Ins. Comp's – Fixed Annuities   Fixed Indexed Annuities   REITs, Futures, etc.
                                                  Ins. Comp's – Var. Ann's

1. Principal is Guaranteed
2. Interest is guaranteed
3. Term is guaranteed
4. Penalties for early withdrawal

1. Starts with Principal Protection
2. Links interest to an external market index
3. Penalties for early withdrawal
4. Not invested directly in market

1. Principal is NOT Guaranteed
2. Interest/earnings are NOT guaranteed
3. Term is generally open ended
4. Need TIME to be effective, but how much time is (?)

Potential Interest Over Next 12 Months
1% - 4%

Potential Interest Over Next 12 Months
0% - 20%

Potential Interest/Earnings Over Next 12 Months
-40% ? +40%

34

Safety / Guarantees World

One of the reasons why people put money in certificates of deposit at the bank is because they are choosing one of these three options. Can you name which one? If you choose absolute *safety*, you are right. High growth potential? Forget it. As I write this, you are lucky to receive a 1 percent return on a CD.

In 2008, after Robert Spahn of Paradise Valley, Arizona, died, his children sold his old, rundown house to a couple "as is." When the new owners decided to do some remodeling, the contractor they had hired to do the work began finding cash in the walls. Over the years, Mr. Spahn had stuffed more than $500,000 into cans and hidden them inside the framing of the old house. The courts ruled that the money belonged to Mr. Spahn's heirs (I guess "finders keepers" doesn't work in Arizona). Why did the man hide his money in the walls? Because he didn't trust banks! He wanted to be able to put his hands on his money any time he wanted to (liquidity), and he was afraid that if people knew he had it, they would try to steal it from him, so he hid it in the walls (safety of principal). Obviously Mr. Spahn was not interested in receiving any interest on the cash (growth).

We can have money that is fully liquid in a checking or savings account at the bank. But the returns will be paltry. If we want a better return from the bank, we have to tie up the money in a three-year or five-year CD. Because money has a time value, a five-year CD will yield more than a three-year CD.

The returns of any certificate of deposit will not amount to very much, but at least the principal is guaranteed. If you want more growth potential you will have to forfeit guarantees and take on risk.

Safety, liquidity and growth – pick any two. If we have investments that are safe and liquid, what are we giving up? Growth. It is not always black and white, cut and dried. Some investments can have a measure of all three but with one field being more dominant than the others. Imagine three columns, each with a heading of either "Growth," "Safety," or "Liquidity." Now imagine that an investment is scored based on the percentage of those three attributes. An investment in a growth stock, for example, has a high growth potential, but will it score high in the "Safety" category? Nope. How about liquidity? It will be somewhat liquid but you probably won't be able to write a check on that asset, nor can you press a few buttons on the automated teller machine and have it distributed to you in the form of cash. You must first sell the shares of stock and convert the proceeds into cash. But, unless you are dealing with a qualified account, there is no penalty for early withdrawal (unless of course the value has depreciated). I always make clear to people that equity investments are only really "liquid" if the value has gone up, not down. Yes, you can get your money, but at what cost?

In the "Safety" category, what entities dominate? Banks, the U.S. government and insurance companies. What do banks offer that are completely safe? Savings, checking and CDs. What does the government offer that are completely safe? Treasury bonds, savings bonds, inflation bonds and agency bonds. Agency bonds are issued by Federal National Mortgage Association (Fannie Mae), and the Government National Mortgage Association (Ginnie Mae), both of which are fully backed by the U.S. government, which is a fancy way of saying "fully backed by U.S. tax payers."

What do insurance companies offer that are completely safe? Fixed annuities, Fixed Indexed annuities, and life insurance. Everything in these categories is a known quantity. You know your money is safe from loss and that your principal is guaranteed. You know what your interest rate is and you know that it is guaranteed. You are fully aware of your term and the term is guaranteed. There are no surprises in this category. But to have that safety, you must give up high growth potential. Can you obtain a higher rate of a return with a fixed or fixed indexed annuity than you can with a one-year CD at the bank? Absolutely! Probably three or four times as much and maybe more. And the money is guaranteed safe, too. So what are you giving up? A measure of liquidity. With fixed or fixed indexed annuities, you agree to park your money with the insurance company for a period of time, and agree that if you withdraw more than the proscribed free withdrawal amount before that term, you will pay a penalty for early withdrawal.

Risk / Potential Growth World

Risk world is an exciting place. You never know what will happen. It could be up, it could be down or it could be flat. This up-one-minute-and-down-the-next world does, however, offer more growth potential than the world of safety. Among the denizens of this world are mutual funds, stocks, bonds, variable annuities, and the list goes on. Brokerage houses, such as Merrill Lynch and Smith Barney, call this world home, as well as independent stock brokers. Variable annuities and REITS (Real Estate Investment Trusts) live here too, where earnings are not guaranteed, the term is open-ended. You can hold a stock for five minutes or 50 years and the results could be the same. Average returns can range anywhere from minus 40 percent (or lower) to positive 40 percent (or greater). The more time you have on your side, the more effective money will be in risk world. Over time, the market has shown a positive return of approximately 8 percent. If you go back 50 years, you will find that the S&P 500 index has been up and down, but when you add it all up and taken an average, it will be right there around 8 or 9 percent. Take a 20-year sampling of the market from virtually any period and you will get the same results. What does that tell us? Simply that, despite the risk associated with this world, if *time* is on your side, it is appropriate to have a portion of your wealth at work for you here. So that tells us that, in spite of the risk involved, if you have *time,* it is not inappropriate to have some of your assets in risk world.

Since this world is subject to volatility, is it possible to jump in when prices are low and buy up a lot of shares and then jump out when the market reaches its peak? In other words, buy consistently low and sell consistently high? That would be nice, but no one, not even fortune tellers and palm readers, have been able to pull off that one. If that were possible, Risk World would not be risky, would it? If anyone suggests that they have the ability to time the market, they are delusional or intentionally lying to you. Run.

How about liquidity in this world of Wall Street? In this world, you have a greater measure of liquidity, for example, than you do with an annuity from an insurance company, or CD from a bank. It may take a few hours to liquidate a position in the market, but when you do you are able to receive the full value of the sold shares without paying a penalty. Let me point out again, the value of shares is not guaranteed. So even though they may be "liquid," if they have lost value there is a cost to "liquidate." Most folks don't want to, or won't, sell if shares have lost value. That's why I say equities are only "really liquid" if the value has gone up.

The only exception to that is when you are buying or selling shares within a qualified account, such as a 401(k). In this case, a withdrawal of funds from the account may have a penalty imposed by the IRS for individuals under the age of 59½ and certain tax consequences may apply.

The thing to remember here is that to get growth potential, we give up safety. This is the world also of the unknown. We do not know what earnings will be and there are no guarantees. There are no term obligations here. Term is usually open ended.

Hybrid World

And then we have Hybrid World. A hybrid, as everyone knows, is a combination of two things. In this case, it is a combination of the known and the unknown. In Hybrid World, your principal is guaranteed and term is known. It is a middle world that emphasizes safety and growth potential at the same time. Since the "pick any two" principle applies here also, we are giving up a measure of liquidity in order to have the other two. Hybrid World is a relatively new world, dominated by banks and insurance companies. Chase Manhattan Bank first introduced the Equity Linked Certificate of Deposit in 1987. The idea of the ELCD is to provide a guarantee of principal while allowing a growth rate which is attached to the stock market. They have recently become more widely available as a product to compete with mutual funds and other market-based investments. These are "investments" in which there is no risk because the principal is not directly in the market, but is tied to, or linked with, a market index. The ELCD has a few moving parts. You could be linked to a group of stocks or even a stock index, like the S&P 500, the Nasdaq, or the Dow Jones. When these stocks or indices rise in value, so do the returns, *up to a point*. That cap is determined by the terms of the investment. Why is a cap necessary? It's another tradeoff. The cap is necessary to ensure the safety of your principal.

In the mid 1990s, Insurance companies began to offer annuities that work on the same general principle as the ELCD. You deposit a lump sum, just as you would into the bank, and the insurance company issues you a contract with provisions similar to the ELCD. The product, which became known as a Fixed Indexed Annuity, was first introduced by Keyport Life Insurance Company, now known as Sun Life, in February 1995. The popularity of FIAs seems to soar during bear markets when the reality of market risk hits home. Sales of FIAs totaled more than $30 billion per year between 2009 and 2012, according to a Fixed Annuity Premium Study by Beacon Research. When the product was first introduced, only a few insurance companies offered the FIA. As of this writing, FIAs are offered by 44 different insurance companies.

The main draw of the FIA is that an investor receives the upside potential of the market as reflected by a stock index, such as the S&P 500, and has the contractual guarantee of safety of principal. During the relatively brief time FIAs have been around they have averaged around 6 percent returns with no losses.

What if you put your money into an FIA and change your mind? Remember, to get the benefits of better growth potential along with safety of principal, you sacrificed a measure of liquidity. Most FIAs allow you to withdraw 10 percent per year from the account without penalty, but amounts above that are subject to a penalty for early withdrawal that can start as high as 15 to 20 percent decreasing yearly to zero over the term of the contract, which is typically 10 years or so. There are FIAs that allow for cumulative withdrawals of 20-50 percent! There are also FIAs that have "return of premium" riders that will allow you to "walk away" with your entire premium at anytime with no penalties. Insurance companies have worked very hard in this annuity space to provide safety, a measure of growth, and a certain amount of liquidity.

Know Where Your Money Is

The number one mistake I see people making when they approach retirement is not knowing specifically how their assets are distributed among the three worlds of investment. It would be wise to lay your portfolio out and place it against the matrix of these three categories and determine where you stand as it pertains to risk, safety and liquidity and then ask yourself if that is where you wish to be. This type of exploration is fundamental to basic financial planning.

"Holy cow, I'm taking way more risk than I thought I was," exclaimed one man after a review of his situation. Failing to realize that one's financial security is in jeopardy is how some lost their money in the stock market crash of 2008. If we are standing on a railroad track and there is no train in sight, common sense tells us that one will eventually come along. The wise and sensible course of action would be to get off the tracks. I'll say it one more time: ***DON'T TAKE ON MORE RISK THAN NEEDED IN RETIREMENT!!***

Chapter Five

Putting Your Financial Ship in Order

When I am called upon to speak at seminars and educational workshops, I love to poll the audience as to what they expect the economy will do in the next 10 years. Some of the answers I get are interesting. The "doomsayers" warn that we should all be stocking up on canned goods and be prepared for the next Great Depression, which will, by the way, make the one of the 1930s look like a party. Then there are those who feel that we are on the cusp of a bright new era of world peace and unilateral prosperity where third-world nations will emerge and end poverty, the Middle East will stop squabbling, and science will cure all disease.

Of course, no one knows for sure what will happen in the next 10 minutes. But when it comes to the stock market, it will have to either go up, down or sideways. I will sometimes put up a slide or draw a sketch on the easel to illustrate those possibilities and then make it a multiple choice question by a show of hands. Sideways always wins.

Finding Safe Harbor in Retirement

WHICH WAY IS THE MARKET GOING?

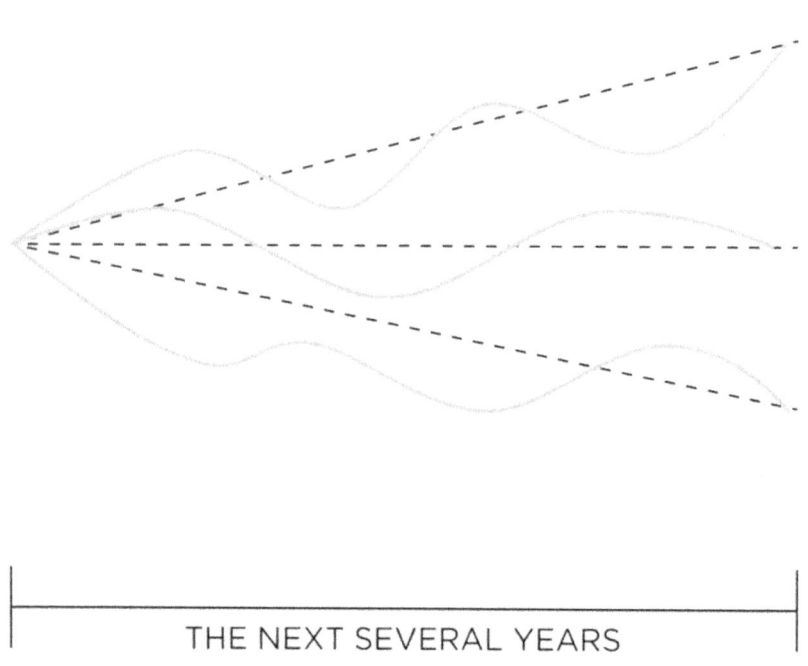

THE NEXT SEVERAL YEARS

Hope for the Best; Prepare for the Worst

    Since we don't know and can't know the future, I'm going to go out on a limb here and make the following statement: Good financial planning, in fact good planning of any type of endeavor, calls for hoping for the best while you remain prepared for the worst. Especially is this true of folks who are approaching retirement. Ask yourself, "What will happen to my portfolio if we get the worst?" If you are retired, the answer you want to be able to give is "It doesn't matter." In other words, I will be in good shape regardless of which of these three possible outcomes happens. Do you need the market to do well for your retirement to succeed? Then you may find it a bit hard to sleep at night. And yet, when you park your entire nest egg with a brokerage firm, you are, for the most part, in that category. You are relying on the upward movement of the market for your financial security. Brokerage firms are, remember, in the world of growth which takes on risk to accomplish it.

When we talk about the "worst" days of the stock market, what always comes to mind? The Great Depression? Sure. The reason why "The Great Depression" is capitalized is because it is iconic as the worst economic period ever to be recorded in history. When you look at a chart showing the years that followed the Great Depression of the 1930s, you can see the pattern of recovery followed by a decline, followed by another recovery, followed by another decline. The graph looks like teeth of a saw blade. Each up is followed by a jagged down. True, that's just the way markets behave and those are only lines on the paper, but those were real personal fortunes that were lost and remained that way during those down periods. The U.S. economy did not return to its 1929 GNP for over a decade, and still had an unemployment rate of about 15 percent in 1940. While that was better than the 25 percent unemployment of 1933, it shows the overall weakness of the recovery from the Great Depression. There was slow recovery through the mid 1930's but international events prevented any huge recovery. By 1938 war in Europe looked likely and hopes of a recovery were waning. It took World War II and the massive return to industrial production to finally end the Great Depression and it is fair to say that it took Wall Street over 20 years to regain the levels of 1929.

Anything can happen in an economy. What are the chances of another Great Depression? No one knows, but no one rules it out, either. When I ask that question of audiences, I seldom hear, "No way!" or, "Absolutely not!" The most common answer is that it will probably happen again one day. The more layers you peel back on the causes of the market crash of 2008 the more you realize that the measures that were put in place to prevent another Great Depression simply don't measure up to their press clippings. If we have learned anything about ships since the epic sinking of the Titanic in 1912, it is not to give any vessel the label, "unsinkable."

Bear Markets and Recoveries

There are many things we can learn by looking at the past, but one of them is not what will happen in the future. I am amused to see how some stock market analysts pore over the least little bump and wiggle of an historical chart of a stock's movement and proclaim that these up and down movements can forecast what will happen in the long run. All the history we can collect will only tell us what happened in the past. It is a great indicator, however, of how we should behave in the face of the market's inherent unpredictability.

What can we learn from looking at the past? Several things. We learn that since 1929 there have been 16 periods of what we call **bear markets**. A bear market is defined as a 20 percent or greater decline in the S&P 500 Index.

We also know by looking at the past that bear markets occur at the rate of one every 4.8 years. We observe that the average depth of a bear market is a 38.24 percent decline in the S&P and that the average bear market lasts for 17 months. The average time we spend making up for the losses of a bear market is 60 months.

Now if we could just see into the future, we could buy as many shares of as much stock as we possibly could just before a bull market begins and then cash out when it peaks. We would be rich beyond our wildest imaginings and every talk show host would want to interview us. Wouldn't that be nice? Rich *and* famous!

I think it's interesting to look at what I call the **Break-Even Period.** That's the length of time it takes to regain the ground lost after a bear market. Some recessions have been very brief but very deep. Remember 1987? That little bear market only lasted three months, but the S&P lost a whopping 33.5 percent! The recovery period was about two years. The bear market that lasted from March 2000 to October 2002 saw the S&P plunge 49.1 percent! It lasted 31 months and took 87 months to recover.

Since part of my job description is to know what is happening on Wall Street, the flat-screen TV on the wall of my office is usually tuned to the financial channels. Many of us who follow the market probably remember when the ticker headline at the bottom of the TV screen announced the trading results on September 29, 2008. We watched, open mouthed, as the DJIA lost a record 777 points in one day, which as of this writing, still stands. With perfect hindsight we can now see that bear market actually started in October 2007, and lasted throughout March 2009. It was the steepest nosedive since the Great Depression, with the S&P 500 losing an incredible 56.7 percent.

Let's say you had your entire fortune tied up in the stock market then. You would have felt pretty confident on October 9, 2007, when the DJIA peaked at its pre-recession all-time high of 14,164.43. By March 5, 2009, however, it bottomed out at 6,594.44. Your mood would have been somber indeed. By February 1, 2013, however, the Dow had struggled back to 14,000 and even crested above the 15,000 a few months later. Here's the question. Were you back to even? Not by a long shot!

Losses Can Be Deceiving

Losses can be very deceiving. I will sometimes ask audiences the following question: "If I have $100,000 in the stock market and the market goes down 50 percent, how much does the market have to go back up again for me to break even?" The first answer I get is usually 50 percent. It's at that point that I put my hands in my pockets and look at my shoe tops for a few seconds to let the light bulb get a little brighter. And it inevitably does.

On the surface 50 percent sounds like the right answer, doesn't it? I mean, you lost 50 percent, you got back 50 percent; you're back where you started! Right? Not really. Think about it for a moment. When the market goes down 50 percent, you get a new starting point for the climb back up. You no longer have $100,000 in your account. When the market finally bottoms, you have to start the ride back up with $50,000, not $100,000. So how much would the market have to go up for you to get back to the $100,000 you started with? If it only went up 50 percent and stopped, you would be credited with only half of $50,000, or $25,000. That means that you only have $75,000, right? That's not breaking even.

To get back to even the market has to go up another 25 percent. In other words, the answer to the original question is 100 percent, not 50. That is why it is so critical to avoid investment losses. When you experience large losses you have less to invest and it takes longer to get back to even.

In the illustration, we used 50 percent to make the math easy. But if you lost 50 percent of your money in the stock market, you can probably kiss goodbye the thought of ever getting even. It's what is called an unsustainable loss. Think about it. Even **if** the market gained 10 percent per year (which is highly unlikely) and you were 100 percent invested, it would take seven years (seven instead of 10 because of compounding) to get back to square one.

To make the point even easier to grasp, I will sometimes take four quarters and place them on the table and say, "Here you are before the market crashed. Then you lost 50 percent." I take two of the quarters away.

"The market rebounds 50 percent." I put one quarter back, since that is 50 percent of what was lost. "It will take a 100 percent market gain to get back what was lost," I say as I put the other quarter on the table. That mental picture is hard to forget.

Average Returns Vs. Actual Returns

It's extremely important to understand the difference between average returns, and actual returns. If you would have invested $10,000 per year into the S&P 500 from 1995 through 2002, you would have invested $80,000 over eight years.

The average annual rate of return over that eight year span was 10.63 percent! Not bad right? But, your ACTUAL account balance would have been $81,865. That equates to an ACTUAL annual return of .051 percent, yuk!! How does that happen? It's really just simple math. The total of all returns for the S&P 500 for that eight year period was 85.03 percent. Simply divide that number by eight, and the ANNUAL rate of return equals 10.63 percent.

By the end of 1999 your account would have been worth $102,773. Awesome!! But remember what happened in 2000, 2001, & 2002? Yep, you guessed it. The S&P 500 was down over 46 percent. So by the end of 2002, your account value dropped to $81,865. Yep, that equals an .051 percent ACTUAL annual rate of return over that eight year period. I know 10.63 percent sure sounds nice but remember, it's not what you make, it's what you keep that counts!! The good old boys on Wall Street sure have some sneaky ways of bending the truth don't they?

James D. Stillman

LOSSES & RECOVERY

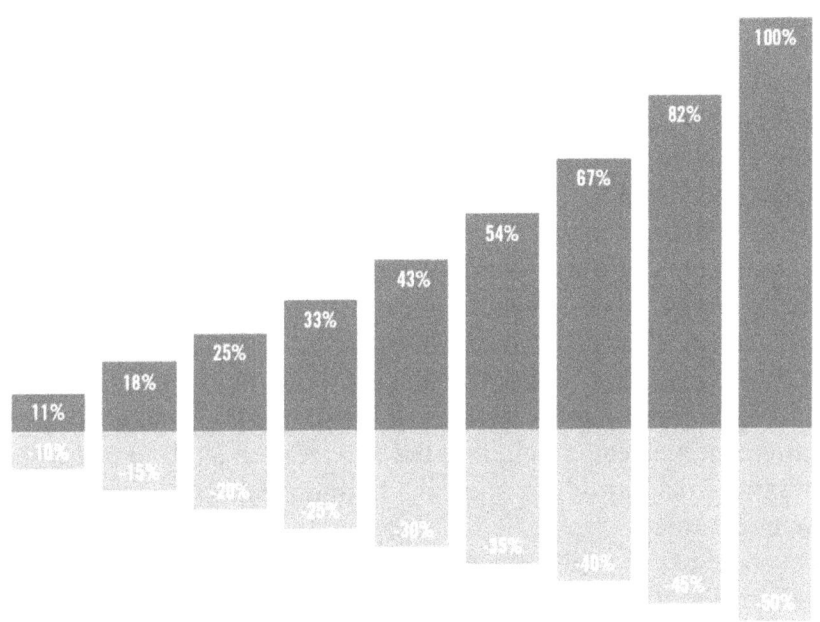

Earlier in this book we focused the bright light of investing truth on the so-called "4 Percent Rule" and explained why it is no longer a valid principle of retirement planning in this modern age. One of the reasons why the formula no longer works has to do with the euphoric bull market of the 1990s. Another doctrine of investing that brokerage firms tout as being an irrefutable truth is "Buy and Hold."

The idea behind the "buy and hold" strategy is to simply keep the faith, hold the wheel, don't bail out, stay put, hold the fort, don't give up the ship (add other similar metaphors here). The idea is that, even if the market goes down, don't worry; it will bounce back. During the 1990s that was true. In those days, any dip in the Dow would be filled in within a year or so and it was off to another record high. But that just stopped happening after the Dot Com bubble burst in 2000. Two crashes, two long bear markets, and a "lost decade" later, and we have to come to the sobering conclusion that what worked a quarter century ago simply does not work now. When it comes to investing philosophy, what is true during a protracted bull market is simply not true during other times. If the new normal for the market is stormy and volatile, then it's time for strategies that will not allow losses that could sink your retirement ship.

Reverse Dollar Cost Averaging

In chapter two of this book we discussed the principle of Dollar Cost Averaging and how it benefits a younger investor. You can literally do no wrong if you keep pumping regular, steady contributions into a market-based investment. But the same force that propels you when you are young and in savings mode, can ruin you when you are older and withdrawing your money from that account. When you retire, it's the reverse side of the coin. Now you are making systematic ***withdrawals*** instead of systematic deposits. Every time you make that withdrawal, you are selling shares, not buying them. Since you need the same amount each week to provide you with a paycheck in retirement, you can't wait until the market is on a roll to make your withdrawals. That would be nice, but timing the market is impossible, as we have already established. If you could time the market, then the higher share prices would mean more cash for fewer shares, leaving the remainder of the account to continue growing. The fact is, if you are on a fixed income and the source of that income is from withdrawals taken from a market-based account, you have no choice but to sell those shares – even during a bear market. That's *reverse* dollar cost averaging and the sting of it can be really painful.

The Solution

The solution is to move your money to a safer place after you retire – a place where you can have a stable, acceptable gain, a guarantee of no losses, and, if possible, a guaranteed lifetime income. This is one way, as the title of this book suggests, to find a safe and secure harbor in retirement – an environment that will eliminate the harrowing pitch and roll of a volatile stock market and make your retirement worry-free. In other words, a retirement plan that will succeed in ***any economy!***

Chapter Six

Planning the Risk Out of Retirement

Approaching retirement can be a scary proposition for some. It's like stepping into a completely new world. The umbilical weekly paycheck is gone and so is the day-to-day activity that came with it. Now we start relying on other sources for our income. That can be frightening if those income sources aren't sufficiently forthcoming. Stepping into uncharted territory is risky business and planning and preparation can mitigate that risk

My wife, Judy, and I learned a life lesson about preparedness and planning in our early 30's when we "retired" and embarked on a two-year sailing adventure aboard our 35-foot-long sailboat, *Second Wind* – a trip that would take us far from our Milwaukee, Wisconsin home. We began by planning our itinerary. Our ultimate destination was the powder- blue water of the Bahamas. But to get there from the heartland of America would require threading our way through the Great Lakes, across New York State on the Erie Barge Canal System, down the Hudson River from Troy, New York, to New York City. From there we intended to turn left and make our way to Long Island Sound via the East River and head for Martha's Vineyard off the coast of Massachusetts. We would then sail down the east coast to Florida, cross through the Okeechobee Waterway to Fort Myers, Florida, on the Gulf Coast. We planned to sail north to Clearwater, Florida, then south past the Florida Keys and then over to the Bahamas. It was an ambitious plan.

Finding Safe Harbor in Retirement

I had learned to sail on Wisconsin lakes as a teenager. But there is a big difference between day sailing and what we were about to do. We would be traversing four of the five Great Lakes and making our way through the twists and turns of dozens of connecting waterways, locks and bridges, not to mention the long stretches of the open Atlantic Ocean and the Intracoastal Waterway. The boat would be our home for the next two years. The living space on *Second Wind* was cramped – comparable to that of a small camper – but adequate for two people if both were tidy. I began planning years before our departure to make sure we had enough equipment and provisions for the journey and, as it turned out, every square inch of space was needed. Preparing for the trip was enjoyable to me. I suppose careful planning is just in my chip. I also had a passion to achieve my dream, which gave me great incentive. Judy and I both agreed that getting ready for the unknown was part of the adventure. Judy was 25 and I was 31 when we "retired." As you can imagine, we were forced to become very thrifty and expert planners at such a young age. We had put aside a certain amount of money for our journey. When the money ran out, it would be back to work. I often reflect on that when planning income strategies for retirees. We knew when the money ran out we would return to the workaday world. For retiring seniors, however, that is not an option. The finite resources they have saved up for their retirement must last them a lifetime.

Judy and I budgeted carefully from a standpoint of both money and time. We figured it would take us approximately two years and $42,000 to make the leisurely trip to Florida, the Bahamas and back. Remember, this was back in 1985, and I wanted to allow for all the contingencies I could think of, so I read everything I could get my hands on about our route. Being prepared for all the potential dangers was paramount.

The life lessons we learned from our sailing adventure were these:

- Planning properly does prevent most unpleasant circumstances but not all of them.
- Proper preparation enables you to cope with unpleasant circumstances you can't prevent.
- The unexpected ***will*** happen no matter how much you plan and prepare.

- When unanticipated events do occur, being prepared is still much better than being unprepared.

The "Old Salt"

The first unanticipated difficulty we experienced happened as we sailed into the area of New York City. After making it through the Great Lakes, we took down our mast in Tonawanda, New York, and motored through the Erie Canal, then we motor-sailed down the Hudson River past West Point heading toward New York City. It was when we were alongside New York City near the mouth of the Hudson that we learned a thing or two about tides, and the vicious currents that they can cause.

Our first lesson in this regard came when we tied up for the night at a marina just north of the Statue of Liberty. We were asleep in our berths when I was awakened by the sensation that our boat was listing to one side. I stumbled to the companionway and looked out to discover the water level had dropped about five feet and we were heeled over about 10 degrees. That meant that the tide had gone out and our keel was probably resting on the muddy bottom. A few hours later, when the tide came back in and we were afloat again, we moved *Second Wind* to a deeper slip, and I figured I needed to do some more reading about tides. A fellow sailor came by and saw me poring over the pilot book. He had a salt-and-pepper gray beard, kind eyes and a weathered face.

"Had much experience with tides?" he asked. He had either witnessed our encounter from the night before, or he had seen the words, Milwaukee, WI, on our stern. Either way, he knew that we were green in this area of sailing. We were lake sailors, and lakes don't have tides. I told him we were planning on leaving in the morning to sail up the East River, through the narrows called Hell's Gate on the upper end of that tidal strait.

"Let me give you kids a word of advice," said the kindly old man whom Judy and I would later nickname "the old salt." "Study your tide charts or you will not make it through Hell's Gate," he warned, explaining that if we didn't time it properly, our sailboat's auxiliary engine would not have enough power to overpower the currents and we would find ourselves in a bit of trouble. Tide charts, I learned, are different for each area of the country and can be picked up at just about every marina. They provide precise information about the time and depths of each tidal change, and even the velocity of the current in some places. We would need this information more than we realized.

We spent the rest of the next day and into the night learning about the local currents and tides, figuring out just how to time our departure. As I lay, propped up in my bunk, I read all about the gravitational attraction of the sun and moon and how they cause the waters of the ocean to swell and recede at different parts of the earth. There are short periods of calm water called "slack tides" that occur between the tidal shifts. Hell's Gate, I learned, could be as calm as a lake during these "slack tides." Then, two hours later, the roiling current would teach the skipper of a small boat like ours how this little stretch of water got its name! But thanks to our bearded friend, and our careful planning, we made it through Hell's Gate without incident and emerged into the calmer waters of Long Island Sound headed for Massachusetts. Although it has been decades since our sailing adventure, Judy and I often talk about the experience with the "old salt" and things he taught us. It was during this interval that I came to the conclusion that there is no substitute for hands-on experience when it comes to navigating treacherous waters and that planning and preparation are as necessary to new adventures as a map is to a traveler, or a chart is to a boater.

Knowledge and Application

Just like successfully maneuvering through Hell's Gate, planning the risk out of retirement starts with knowledge but ends with applying what you've learned. When I speak about financial planning to audiences, I always like to make the point, that knowledge is useless if not applied. In the case of the two young and intrepid sailors mentioned above, we had to start way at the bottom rung of the knowledge ladder. When it came to tides, we didn't know what we didn't know. Recognizing one's need for knowledge is the first step to obtaining it. I love the quote by former president Woodrow Wilson: "I not only use all the brains that I have, but all I can borrow." Wise man! I personally have a strong belief that "all of us is smarter than any one of us". Woodrow Wilson recognized the limits of his own knowledge and he knew how prudent it is to take advantage of the experience of others. When it comes to retirement income planning, some fail to recognize their need for education. They remain unaware of the potential pitfalls that await them in retirement until they encounter them first hand. That's called "learning the hard way," and it is the most expensive way to learn. What follows are common planning mistakes some make and how to avoid them:

Relying Too Much on Social Security - Underestimating how much income you will need in retirement is chronic among Americans. Would it surprise you to learn that in 2013, among Social Security beneficiaries, 23 percent of married couples and about 46 percent of unmarried persons relied on Social Security for 90 percent of their income? The average monthly Social Security benefit for a retired worker was about $1,230 at the beginning of 2012. That's just a little above the poverty level set by the U.S. Department of Health and Human Services ($11,490 per year for a single person in 2013). Social Security retirement benefits are based on three major factors: your current age, your age when you begin receiving benefits, and your past earnings. To squeeze the most possible juice from the Social Security turnip, you must delay taking your benefits until age 70. Let's say that you contributed enough into the system to get the maximum. The rules as of 2013 say you could get $2,533 per month if you retired at your full retirement age (Full retirement age is 66 for those born after 1942 and 67 if you were born after 1960). But in 2013, for example, if you retired at age 62, your maximum benefit would be $1,923. If you retired at age 70 in 2013, your maximum benefit would be $3,350.

Social Security is a guaranteed lifetime income. With the demise of defined benefit pension plans, guaranteed lifetime incomes are an endangered species. The smart thing to do these days, if you can afford to do it, is to wait until you are age 70 before taking your Social Security. You are, of course, free to stop working and start taking your Social Security benefits anytime between the ages of 62 and 70. But the days when you could expect to get full benefits at the magic age of 65 are gone.

Before you make any decisions on Social Security, consult the Social Security Administration Website, www.ssa.gov. It is a treasure trove of information that can help you gauge to what extent Social Security will cover your expenses when you retire. Finally, I recommend that you consult a knowledgeable retirement income specialist to make sure the options you choose harmonize with the rest of your financial picture.

In 1940, the life expectancy of a 65-year-old was almost 14 years. In 2013, it was more than 20 years. And that's ***average!*** The way life expectancy tables work, the longer you live, the longer you are expected to live. If you make it to age 75, for example, you are expected to live to age 87. You can credit advances in medicine, seatbelts, or more people kicking the tobacco habit, the fact is we are living longer as a society.

Why is that important? Because when it comes to deciding when to take your Social Security, there is a breakeven point to consider. If you outlive your life expectancy you will want the highest possible Social Security check, right? That means waiting as long as possible (up to age 70) to collect it. As of this writing, the amount you collect increases by 8 percent per year. Two exceptions to this, of course would be (a) if you are in poor health and don't expect to live long, or (b) you need the money.

I can already see the wheels turning in some of your minds. If I wait until age 70, how many years will it take for me to recover the passed over benefits? Aha! That is the breakeven point. Some may say, "If it takes me 15 years to break even after waiting until 70 to begin taking my Social Security benefits, and my life expectancy is judged to be only 82, why should I wait?" Well, for one thing, those tables are just averages and estimates based on statistics. You probably won't die exactly when you are supposed to according to some table. It will be earlier or later – hopefully later. So unless you have a special reason (illness or emergency), and unless you have a side fund growing at better than 8 percent interest, it would be better to use that pool of money as opposed to tapping into Social Security early.

Please remember, waiting until you are age 70 is a good decision ***as a general rule.*** There is much to consider and each case is different. Spousal continuance is a factor. If a wife waits until full retirement age, for example, she can collect her full spousal benefit (equal to half of her husband's full retirement benefit) and then wait until age 70 to collect her own maximum retirement benefit. At 70, it will be roughly 65 percent larger than were she to take it early. So much depends on how badly you need the money now, compared to how worried you are about outliving your savings. Another very good reason for the highest paying spouse to delay Social Security, is legacy planning at death for the remaining spouse. If the highest paying spouse dies first (typically the husband) then the remaining spouse would drop her Social Security, and take over the higher payments of her husband.

Your financial advisor should be able to guide you in this area (if not, find a new advisor!) At JDS Wealth Management Corp. we have a program called Social Security Analyzer that helps determine the best possible Social Security strategy. *We highly encourage folks to develop a guaranteed income strategy in combination with social security to maximize both!*

In doing research for this book, I found it interesting to look at the actuarial tables used by Social Security. You will find them at www.http://www.ssa.gov/oact/STATS/table4c6.html. It gets very specific and detailed as to how much longer you will live once you reach a certain age. For example, if you are a woman who has just turned 66 the odds of your dying in the next year, knowing nothing else about you, are .012, or about 1 in 80. Your life expectancy is 66+19.3 = 85.3. But that's an *average*. In other words, half of all 66-year-old women will live to less than 85 but fully half will live to be even older. In my view, the government tends to underestimate how long you will live because the data they are using is from 2007. Life expectancy has gone up since then.

Not knowing your number - One of the most frequently asked questions I hear is, "When can I retire?" The answer, of course, depends on two things: (a) How much do you need in the way of income when you retire and (b) from what sources will your income come and how much will they provide. Some clients are pleasantly surprised to learn that, based on the data from those two collection points, they could have already retired and done so comfortably. For others, however, it is a different story. Either they don't have the resources to retire now and continue the lifestyle to which they have become accustomed (and would like to continue), or they have yet to arrive at point A – How much income they will need in retirement.

I am reminded of that ING commercial featuring a dog-walker named Clark who is strolling down the street carrying a large orange number under his arm. The big orange number is, of course, the amount of money he estimates he needs to have in reserve before he retires. In the commercial, he meets a man who is trimming hedges. Resting on the hedge to his right is the word "Gazillion." The commercial's point is "know your number." How much will you need in income? How much do you have in savings? You are the only one who can answer both those questions.

Just as our "old salt" helped Judy and I understand what knowledge we needed to make it through Hell's Gate in our 35-foot sailboat on our way to Martha's Vineyard, a competent retirement income planner can help you arrive at your number. It is never too late to start planning for retirement, even if it's right around the corner. But the earlier the better!

Failing to establish or follow a budget – One of the most elementary financial mistakes I see retirees make is living without a budget. Take my word for it - If you don't track your spending, you *will* overspend. I know it is difficult for some of you "free spirits" out there who like to fly by the seat of your pants and make impulsive decisions, but I urge you to find a way to have a budget and stay within the confines of it as best you can.

Sometimes we have to trick ourselves. I know one person who keeps a "bogus" check register. When she deposits money into her checking account she records $50 less than she actually put into the account. She says that forces herself to think she has less money than she actually has. I couldn't do that, because I would always be doing the math in my head and figuring in the difference. But it works for her.

One couple I know uses plastic sliding drawers in the office of their home to "pay their bills" in advance at the beginning of each month. They write the checks at the beginning of the month, stuff them in the envelope, deduct the money from the account as they go, and then mail the envelopes each week according to due date. That one would also drive me crazy. I just pay the bills electronically as I get them. But it works for them.

You only have to have a rudimentary understanding of computers these days to understand how to use one of the many budgeting software programs that have become available in the last decade or so. You can buy them at your local office supply store or you can order them online. Manufacturers that come to mind are Quicken, AceMoney, YNAB (You Need a Budget), Microsoft Money, Simple Home Money Management and ICash. Most of them cost less than $50 and some of them are free. The point is, you don't have to be super-smart or spend a lot of money to establish a budget and adjust your lifestyle to conform to it.

Drawing on savings too readily - As a kid, I remember my parents gave me a glass piggy bank. I put change in it until it was about half-full and then I couldn't stand it. I would get a paper clip and wiggle the money back out of the bank and spend it. Some retirees make the mistake of dipping into their Social Security benefits or retirements too soon and fail to reap their full benefits and potential. Like me with my piggy bank, they are swapping immediate gratifications for long term rewards. To compound the error (pardon the pun) the coins in that glass pig weren't growing at interest. Retirement accounts are (or should be) and Social Security benefits, as previously discussed in this chapter, increase by 8 percent each year you defer claiming them.

I am reminded of that nauseating commercial on television where people scream at the camera, "It's my money and I want it NOW!" I suppose it is human nature to think that way for some, but my advice is to fight the knee-jerk reaction to take away tomorrow's money unless you absolutely have to have it for today. By showing a little patience and restraint, retirees can realize much more income later in their life when it may be needed more urgently to offset other unforeseen expenses.

Not understanding inflation. Retirement plans can be derailed by inflation. It is not uncommon, however, to see many retirement plans missing that crucial piece of the planning puzzle. From what I read, it is statistically probable that a person retiring at age 65 will live at least two more decades. If inflation continues at the steady 3 percent rate that it has historically maintained, that person's purchasing power will be cut in half by the end of those two decades. I see some retirees wearing rose-colored glasses in this respect. That is, some may be making plans for the future based on overly optimistic projections that do not figure in the erosive effects of inflation. This can lead them to spend too much which can leave them in the lurch down the road. Because they lack an understanding of the impact of inflation, some people begin using their retirement income resources too early and risk reaping the negative consequences of running out of money in their old age.

The cost of nearly everything we buy goes up with time. For example, with 3 percent inflation, an item that costs $100 today would cost $134.39 in 10 years. In 15 years, the same item would cost $155.80. Put another way, the value of today's $100 will be only

$64.19 in 10 years. Forewarned is forearmed, as the saying goes. If we know what to expect, we can plan for it. Let's say, for example, that you know that you will need $60,000 for your first year of retirement. How much money will you need in 20 years to maintain the same lifestyle and keep the same purchasing power, assuming an annual inflation rate of 3 percent? If the value of $60,000 will be $33,220 in 20 years, then you will need $108,336 in 20 years to match the purchasing power of $60,000. Now you can factor that into your planning.

While all the above is true, there exists unwarranted hysteria about inflation, too. Figuring in the runaway inflation that marked the late 1970s and early 1980s into a projection could significantly skew the numbers of an inflation projection. In those days, interest rates briefly rose to upwards of 18 percent or more before things settled.. Also, it is likely that a retiree's expenses will decrease. The U.S. Bureau of Labor Statistics has published figures showing the spending requirements from age 45 to age 75 will be approximately 45 percent lower. Worse than not planning for inflation at all is getting too worked up about it and placing more assets than necessary into aggressive investments to compensate. When it comes to accounting for inflation in financial planning, 3 percent is a reasonable number. Since we cannot predict the future, there is no hard and fast rule. Besides, much still depends on the individual and his or her lifestyle choices. I find it interesting to note that the central banks of some countries project an even more modest inflation rate of below 3 percent.

Becoming a bank for family members - My parents taught me many things as I was growing up. My father taught me the value of hard work and my mother taught me the value of a kind heart. When I wanted something that cost more money than I had in my pockets (and most things did), I never went to Dad. I knew what the answer would be. Yes with an asterisk. The asterisk was that I had to work for it and he could invent plenty of jobs for me to do around the house. My mother, on the other hand would always say no, which meant yes if you ask nicely two or three times. Once she turned her back to me, looked over her shoulder, and asked lightheartedly, "Do you see the word "BANK" printed on my back?" That usually meant that I was pressing my luck with that last request.

Many of the baby boom generation find themselves in the unique position of caring for "boomerang" children, so called for their propensity to return home after a failed relationship. While that is going on, these same folks sometimes end up becoming caregivers and providers for their aging parents. This has led to the term "the sandwich generation," since they are financially squeezed between two these obligations. These same boomers can even sometimes become caregivers for a third generation when there are grandchildren from the failed relationship are added to the mix. Carol Abaya, who writes and lectures on the subject of the sandwich generation, has coined the expression "the club sandwich generation" to describe this group. These caregivers caught in the middle may well wonder, as did my mother, if the word "BANK" is written on their backs because of the drain on their finances.

As the social fabric of the country changes there are more grandparents who are raising grandchildren and multigenerational homes are more common than ever. Obviously, this can be just one more threat to one's retirement picture. Giving or lending money to family members, particularly if that money is critical to your retirement savings program, is just one more threat to your financial future. I have seen good-hearted parents dip time and again into their nest eggs to pay the rent for a child who lost his or her job. Some find themselves in the awkward position of being co-signers on a loan that both the bank and the child assured them they would probably never be asked to actually pay on. But that co-signature means what it says, as some find out the hard way.

I have seen some of my clients who are grandparents end up paying, not only for their children's education, but also for the education of their grandchildren. With the cost of a four-year university education rising above flood level, this can endanger even the healthiest of retirement programs.

In my view, too many retirees compromise their futures by pouring money down these black holes. Children need to support themselves. I know this is easy to say and hard to do, especially if you are large-hearted. And there may be circumstances in which there are no alternatives available. But if you are the goose that lays the golden eggs and you are gasping for air, it will serve no one for the choking continue. Your first financial obligation **must be** your own support and stability. If you are the one who always bails everyone out when they are in trouble, who is going to bail you out? You may be doing your children a favor by emulating my father. Even if you have the money in your pocket or in your checkbook, don't be so quick to release it. Have them try to find their own solution first. You may be surprised at how resourceful you have taught them to be. I think the psychologists call it "tough love." It is often the best kind.

Proper Tax Planning – One big mistake I see people make over and over again is thinking that their tax preparer is also a tax planner. That could be the case, but more often than not it isn't. You usually see your tax preparer once per year. Those who prepare our tax returns are professionals, no doubt, but their main job is to get the correct numbers in the right boxes. They want to make sure that the tax return is in compliance with the tax code. If you usually see them in March and April, you are one of hundreds that are coming in for the same reason. They are probably to rushed to offer tax planning advice at that time of year, even if that were their specialty.

How do you know if your tax preparer is a tax planner? Just call up and ask for an appointment to go over your tax return line item by line item and make sure you are getting the best deal possible from the IRS. See what the response is. Or ask, "Are there some opportunities that I am not taking advantage of to avoid paying more than my fair share of taxes?"

Is there anything more annoying than paying tax on your Social Security income! You paid when it went in and now you have to pay more taxes when it comes out? What do we call that? Double taxation! You bet! Remember, tax *evasion* is against the law but tax *avoidance via tax planning* is not. In fact, the IRS provides step by step instructions on how to avoid paying more than your fair share of taxes. You just have to know where to look for these instructions and a fully-trained tax planning professional will know exactly where to look. Take Social Security taxes for example. When it was instituted in 1935 Social Security benefits were not taxed. Then in 1984 under the presidency of Ronald Regan the Congress required single taxpayers earning more than $25,000 per year, and married couples filing jointly earning more than $32,000 per year, to pay taxes on up to 50 percent of their Social Security benefits. .

In 1993 under President Bill Clinton, a new law was passed that provided that taxes could be imposed on 85 percent of benefits for single filers with incomes of more than $34,000, and for couples with annual incomes of $44,000 or more. However, the IRS code allows for strategies that can limit or even eliminate Social Security taxes in some circumstances.

In the case of one couple, we were able to reduce their tax liability from $5,756 down to $2,056. So how much does that save them each year? About $3,700 bucks. How did we do that? Simply by eliminating **phantom income** from their tax return. Phantom income is, for example, returns on investments that are plowed right back into the investment but is taxed as if it were flowing into the checking account to be spent. This is known as 1099 income. Interest, dividends, etc. that have to be reported as income whether you use the money or not. In many instances this reportable income causes extra taxes on Social Security income. In one case, a retired couple, both receiving Social Security, had $16,536 in fully taxable, reportable income on their previous year's tax return.

"How much are you going to spend of that money?" I asked them.

"None of it," they replied. We are going to plow that back into our investment."

The amount was just enough to kick them over into a category where they were required to pay taxes on $28,399 of their Social Security income. It was to their advantage on several levels to move that asset to a tax deferred account where the income was not considered taxable by the IRS. We were not able to completely eliminate the taxes due on their Social Security, but we were able to reduce it from $5,723 per year down to around $2,000. Paying taxes on only $8,400 of their Social Security felt a lot better than paying taxes on $28,399.

I heard an illustration on phantom income that went something like this:

A mother says to her child, "Why is the shower running? Are you taking a shower?"

The child replies: "No. I have it running just in case I need to take one." At that point my mom would have cracked me across the head, told me how stupid that was, told me to stop wasting water, and ordered me to "go turn off the damn shower before your father comes home!"

We have enough to pay in the way of taxes that pour down on us on all sides without paying taxes on money we receive on paper but do not spend. These usually show up in the form of gains from investment portfolios, dividends and capital gains.

Think about all of your money in three buckets. The first bucket is money you need today. When should you pay tax on money you need today? Well, probably today, right? The next bucket is money you need later. You don't need it right now, but you might need it a few years from now. When should you pay tax on that money? Later, when you need it, right? If you are fortunate, you may have money that you will never need. When should you pay tax on that? If you answered "never," then you and I are on the same philosophical wave length when it comes to taxes. That's the problem with 1099 phantom income. It is usually money in those last two buckets creating taxes on money we are not using. The way to prevent this from happening is to simply redistribute it.

Failing to consider the impact of taxes, including those incurred from retirement account distributions, can lead to costly surprises for retirees. I know of one retired couple that overlooked the tax implications of pulling money straight from a 401(k) account to finish renovating a home. They wanted to have a house fully paid for. Then when the tax bill for more than $100,000 came, they sat in their paid-for house and actually wrung their hands and wept. All of that could have been avoided with a two sentence question and answer session with a financial advisor. Whatever the financial transaction, including the tax consequences into your calculations will help you avoid the heartache of financial jolts like that.

One of the things I enjoy most about my profession is seeing the smiles on client's faces when they see their taxes reduced. It's even better than that feeling I get on the rare occasions when I find a five-dollar bill in my coat pocket. And after having spent years of seeing those smiles, I have never had one person tell me they were unhappy that they weren't able to contribute that money to Uncle Sam. I have yet to receive a letter that reads: "Dear Jim, I really enjoyed our meeting last week, but I really think I should send this money to the government anyway instead of keep it. You know, Jim, our government needs money and people with money should pay more in taxes if they can."

Nope. Not once do I hear that. If I could see the cartoon thought bubble above their heads when that "tax elimination" realization hits, it would probably have palm trees and a beach inside. I know how they feel.

Basing retirement lifestyle on unrealistic projections – Projections are guesses based on the past as to how an investment will perform in the future. If the decade of the 2000s and beyond has taught us anything, it is that projections can be misleading. During the Wall Street heyday of the 1990s, when the only direction the market could go in was up, financial advisors projected it would remain in that direction for decades to come. Many retirees based their lifestyle expenditures on those unrealistically high expectations, which in turn prompted them to take out more money from their investments than was prudent. One retirement strategy that is gaining in popularity these days is to ensure that all of your *essential* living expenses will be covered by *guaranteed income sources*. Then if a crash occurs, you won't be wiped out. The word "guarantee" seems to be more and more comfortable in the minds of retiring Americans than the word "projection."

Underestimating or ignoring the possibility of long-term care – None of us like to think of ourselves needing long term health care in a nursing home or an assisted living facility, but the facts are the facts. The longer you live the greater the possibility that you will face such an eventuality. Research shows:

- For a couple turning 65, there is a 70 percent chance that one of them will need long-term care. - *Wall Street Journal*
- The average stay in a nursing home for the elderly is between two and three years - *Business Week*
- Of people over the age of 85, some 97 percent will require assistance in the last year of life. - *The LTC Report*
- Over 50 percent of all people entering a care situation are penniless within one year. - *Harvard University*
- In 2012, a private room cost an average of $248 daily, or more than $90,500 annually – *MetLife survey*
- By 2018, a private room will cost over $500/day ($188,000/year). - *LTCIP Academy*

Some overestimate what Medicare will cover. Some assume Medicare will cover all or most long term care costs. This is far from true. Take home health care for example. The cost of hiring someone to come in to help with bathing, toileting and getting dressed is not covered unless you're also receiving nursing care. Help with shopping, meal prep and cleaning is Medicare-covered only if you're receiving hospice care, too. If you need skilled care in a nursing home, Medicare will pay the Medicare-allowed rate for the first 20 days, part of the cost for the next 21 to 100 days and then nothing at all after 100 days. You almost have to have a degree in deciphering to understand what is and what is not covered. You can download the very comprehensive booklet *Medicare & You* from the medicare.gov website, but you will find that Medicare is not help when it comes to covering the actual cost of long term health care in a nursing home or assisted living facility.

Long term care insurance is a solution, but there are problems with it. If you wait too long to buy it (after 65 years of age) it can get expensive. If you buy it early, say in your 40s, or 50s it is more affordable, but it is a use-it-or-lose-it proposition unless you pay big bucks for a "return of premium" rider. If you never need it, your premiums are gone forever. It isn't like life insurance that builds a cash value. It is like car insurance. Your premiums, in most cases, are never returned. But there are new solutions that have become available just recently that may provide a workable solution to this dilemma. These types of programs have come to be known as **"asset-based long term care."** A competent financial advisor who specializes in retirement planning will be able to explain them for you. If you are approaching or in retirement, and your advisor is not up to speed with asset-based long term care strategies, you may find it in your best interests to find another advisor. I have provided a short chapter later on in this book that pertains to asset-based long term care. This stuff will blow you away.

Chapter Seven

The Case for Seeking Professional Financial Advice

    I think it is a mistake to not have the oil changed every 3,000 miles in your car, to skip breakfast and to avoid seeking the help of a financial professional when it comes to planning for retirement.

    I will admit this one is a little self-serving. But like my grandfather said, "What's right is right." You *do* need a financial advisor if you have any assets at all saved up for retirement. Do-it-yourself is good for some things. Minor household repair jobs, maybe. But I don't recommend do-it-yourself surgery or do-it-yourself financial planning. This is especially true when in retirement, and "income planning" is involved. With today's low interest rates on savings, market volatility, the pending bond market crash (we're in a bond bubble), and higher inflation looming on the horizon, it's just no place for a "do it yourselfer" in my opinion. There's just too much at stake, and you only have to screw it up once to mess up the rest of your life. To consult a professional when it comes to your health and your wealth is a sign of intelligence.

    Quite often, it takes the kind of questions a professional will ask to crystallize your thinking regarding what you expect your assets to do for you. When individuals begin thinking about retirement, the burning question often is: "At what age can I retire?" It is a loaded question and the only legitimate answer is, "It depends." Before anyone can answer that question, you have to ascertain several things about your personal financial situation. What are your goals, your dreams, your plans, your required income, your vision of the future? To lay all of those things out in a meaningful way requires the help of a professional. To take that information and use it to come up with a personalized plan of action that is both effective and reasonable will most certainly require the help of a professional – especially these days with things changing at breakneck speed.

Just as you can get advice on your health from virtually every corner these days, the same is true of your wealth. Opinions, both published and non-published, are as ubiquitous as highway billboards. Each one says something different, and they can't all be right, can they? Does it matter to you whether your decisions about money are based on facts and rooted in research? A competent financial advisor will know how to interpret all the esoteric language that goes along with investing and make sense of the financial road ahead in retirement.

Another reason for using a professional financial advisor is that it it enables you to distance yourself emotionally from the decisions required to plan a worry-free retirement. A popular phrase since the advent of smart phones is, "there's an app for that." A financial advisor will be "plugged in" to the many computer programs that have emerged in the last few years. These "apps," or computer programs, have been of immeasurable assistance to retirees who want to know what are the smartest moves to make for a successful retirement.

A word of caution – Just as you wouldn't go to a dentist for an opinion on a heart condition, you also will not find it advisable to seek the advice of a financial advisor until you first determine whether he or she is qualified to advise you in the area in which you need help. Don't hesitate to ask the following questions,

- How long have you been a financial professional?
- How many clients are you currently helping?
- What are your credentials and why should I hire you?
- What does your typical client look like?
- Is there an area of financial planning in which you specialize?

Conflicting Information Overload

In chapter three of this book, I discussed with you several investing myths that people put stock in for one reason or another. One of the myths of the animal kingdom is that ostriches stick their heads in the sand when they sense danger approaching. You have heard that, haven't you? Well, you can put that one in the same category with the indigestible chewing gum and the wart-causing toads. It just isn't so. Zoologists say that the ostrich got this reputation because of the bird's habit of using its beak to dig shallow holes in the loamy soil of Australia in search of food. The bird isn't escaping trouble; it is merely looking for its lunch!

I do believe, however, that people tend to emulate this mythical behavior when they become confused by the overwhelming volume of conflicting financial advice they encounter these days. The syndrome is, "I don't know who is right and who is wrong, so I will just do nothing. I was in an airport recently, looking for something to read on the plane, and I couldn't help but notice how many magazines are devoted to finance. The editors of these periodicals seem to go out of their way to disagree with one another. Below are some actual excerpts:

"*A **buy and hold** approach has done the best over the long run...*" Forbes Magazine 12/03 2010

"***Buy-and-hold*** *doesn't work anymore."* – Money Magazine 03/02/2012

"***Diversify into gold.*** *Some of the wealthiest and most astute managers of money in the world today remain bullish on **gold**.*" Business Insider 10/03/2012

*"Why Warren Buffet Thinks Investing in **Gold is Stupid**"* – Headline, Wall Street Journal 04/18/2013

The tsunami of conflicting financial advice comes at us from all sides. I counted at least 18 channels dealing with finance on cable and satellite TV. There are books, reports, essays, and endless editorials created by Wall Street watchers, much of it self-serving and sensational. Within the financial advisory community, advisors seem to be so polarized in their opinions that you wonder how they could be in the same profession. It is easy to see why a distrusting John Q. Public just closes his eyes and sticks his fingers in his ears. They can't all be right, can they?

Well, yes and no.

Consider this: Doctors sometimes disagree as to how to treat an illness or injury. A friend told me that when he experienced back pain he consulted his family doctor. The family doctor referred him to a neurologist. After a series of X-rays and an MRI, the specialist prescribed muscle relaxers, outfitted him with a back brace, and discussed surgery if the pain did not abate. When he went to a chiropractor, however, he got a completely different recommendation. The chiropractor recommended a series of adjustment treatments and advised him to lose 25 pounds.

"So which opinion did you go with?" I asked.

"Both of them," he replied.

He went on a diet and lost 40 pounds, filled the prescription for muscle relaxers, wore the back brace, went for the chiropractic treatments, and the back pain went away.

Which doctor was right? It could well have been that they both were right, but were merely seeing the problem from different perspectives. The neurologist had been trained to approach problems one way and the chiropractor had been trained in another.

Much of the financial advice circulating today is like that – two schools of thought colliding with each other as to how to achieve the common goal of successful retirement. Insurance agents not certified to offer securities will pound the table and insist that the only way to safeguard assets in retirement is with annuities and life insurance. Stock brokers who are not licensed to offer insurance products and have little knowledge of how they work will pound the table and insist that a market-based approach is the only way to go. The fact of the matter is there is room for both insurance products and equities in a well-balanced retirement plan. In fact, such a mixture is quite often desirable. More and more financial advisors are coming to that conclusion and are becoming Registered Investment Advisors so they can offer both concepts and strategies as each unique situation dictates.

Find a specialist. Retirement income plans, and retirement-savings or investment plans are very different things. With the retirement-savings or investment plans, you are directed to invest, diversify and wait—which is fine if your retirement is 20 or 30 years away. A retirement *income* plan, on the other hand, will require assembling a group of investments, or savings plans that guarantee you an income you cannot outlive and produce steady, long-term growth, with a special focus on safety.

Get a Second Opinion

Getting a medical second opinion is just a smart thing to do. That's what my friend with the back problem did. Getting second opinions when you are dealing with major financial decisions is smart, too – especially if you don't feel comfortable with a particular recommendation. It's okay to trust yourself, too. Can you imagine going to buy a pair of shoes and having the salesperson insist that a pair of shoes fits you when you know that they are a size too small?

"Do you have these in another size?" you ask.

"No. Didn't you see the sign above the door?" says the salesperson. "One size fits all."

"But these hurt my feet," you protest.

"Trust me. They fit you," replies the salesperson.

How ridiculous! I'm sure you will trust your feet, not the bogus advice you are getting from the shoe salesperson. Your feet will tell you immediately whether something fits or not.

There are no one-size-fits-all solutions for financial problems. Some views and modes of thinking in the realm of financial advice-giving simply don't hold up under scrutiny, and they fail to successfully meet the test of logic and clear thinking. If something appears too good to be true, it probably is.

One litmus test as to the legitimacy of financial advice is to follow the money. In other words, if you are given advice that doesn't ring true, or fails to hold up under your own independent research, there is usually a profit motive. Let's face it…profit and personal gain are what make most people get up in the morning and go to work. But a true professional will never pressure you to buy, sign, accept or adopt any strategy, product, plan or program. A true professional will always put your needs ahead of his/her own and you will usually sense that when you have a conversation with that financial advisor. True professionals solve problems. They do not sell goods. True professionals will fully explain any recommendations they may make to your complete satisfaction and will give you choices and alternatives. If you get the feeling that a proposition is one-dimensional and simply doesn't feel right, you may be dealing with a profit-driven salesperson wanting to rack up another sale. If you encounter a situation like that, get other opinions, please. Don't be afraid to "trust your gut"!

Chapter Eight

Steering Clear of Hidden Retirement Dangers

    As the Italian cruise ship, Costa Concordia, was serving dinner to its guests on the evening of January 13, 2012 off the coast of the Tuscan island of Giglio, the hull struck a reef concealed a few feet beneath the surface of the water. As the ship shuddered and lurched, plates of food skittered across the table and fell to the floor and waiters in uniforms reached for handholds to keep their balance. The huge floating hotel with 4,252 passengers aboard began taking on water. Soon the hallways and cabins on the lower decks were flooded as passengers scurried for the lifeboats. The ship floundered and finally came to rest on its side, lying on giant rocks that had remained hidden in the dark water. The captain said he knew the local waters well. He felt sure he could give what is called a "salute" to the people of Giglio. The "salute" meant cruising by close to shore with all the lights on, sounding the ship's horn. He was certain the water was deep enough, but, as the facts would later show, he was way too close to shore.

    When pictures of the half-submerged giant began appearing on television screens and newspapers the next day, the question was repeatedly asked, "How could that happen?" The answer was simple. The captain was taking too much risk and he didn't know the hidden reef was there.

    Our financial ship can be the victim of hidden danger and unseen threats to a worry-free retirement if we aren't vigilant. Some place all their trust in the stock market because it's all they have been taught by their "financial guy." And that's all they have been taught by their "financial guy" because that's all he knows. Don't get me wrong. The stock market is a great way to get you to a certain point in building your retirement nest egg. But once you are there, it is foolish to leave all your eggs in that basket. In my view, and in the view of more and more financial planners who witnessed the carnage of the Market meltdown of 2008 and the subsequent Great Recession, you should **Guarantee your basic income** first. And I am going to go out on a limb here and tell you that that income should come to you in your retirement regardless of what the market does or does not do. I don't believe your *core income* should be based in any way, shape or form on the volatility of the stock market.

In 2008, the ones who caught the worst of it were those who were on the verge of retirement. One couple that came to my office had a little over a million dollars before the crash and ended up with a little over $500,000 after that financial disaster. They had it figured out. Take 5 percent per year and live on it. That's $50,000 per year, they thought to themselves. That plus our Social Security should allow us to continue our present lifestyle for the rest of our lives. But now they were down to a half million and they still needed $50,000 per year in income. "But that will require pulling out 10 percent of our portfolio each year for living expenses!" said the husband. "It's just a matter of time before we run out of money!"

He was right, of course. And still – even after 2008 – I know of several large financial brokerage firms that continue to spread the bogus message that pulling out 4 percent from a diversified portfolio of 50 percent stocks, and 50 percent bonds will ensure you a comfortable income you cannot outlive. Horsefeathers!

These past few years there have been numerous reports that have disputed the 4 percent rule. The Putnam Institute, AARP, T. Rowe Price, The Wharton School of Business, and the Government Accountability Office (GAO) to name a few. They have all come out within the last few years stating that the 4% withdrawal rule did not work in the 2000's, and has a good chance of not working in the future. AARP states that the withdrawal rate should reduce to 2 percent to insure not running out of money, and GAO says after age 65 no more than 25 percent of liquid assets should be in the stock market. The GAO also said that *"retirees need to purchase more annuities."* Why? Because an annuity is the only investment vehicle available that will guarantee lifetime income, period.

Laddering

There are many ways to accomplish this, but allow me to pass along one potential solution. The idea here is to still guarantee you a 5 percent guaranteed lifetime income *without* turning your portfolio into a pension – and still ensure that you don't run aground midway through your golden years. It is called *laddering, or bucketing.*

Take a portfolio and split it into three buckets.

- **Bucket #1** – Put just enough in this bucket to pay out your income for the first five years equivalent to what it would be if you pulled 5 percent of your entire portfolio. Meanwhile the rest of the portfolio is allowed to grow. At the end of the first five years, this account should be worth about zero. Need $12,000 per year? Put around $60,000 in this bucket.
- **Bucket #2** – This bucket takes over where bucket #1 left off. Put just enough money in to provide another five years of income. The key is that while bucket #1 was paying out, buckets #2 and #3 were growing. While bucket #2 is paying out, bucket #3 will have had 10 years of growth. If bucket #3 is invested properly, it should grow enough to replace the first two accounts.
- **Bucket #3** – If this bucket is invested properly, it should take over after the first 10 years and have enough in it to provide the same 5 percent income for life and even provide for inflation protection. Getting the buckets properly balanced and using the right guaranteed strategies is the key. Any competent retirement income specialist should know how to do it.

Income Riders on Fixed Indexed Annuities

Remember back in the good old days when you would work for a company for 25 or 30 years and they would give you a gold watch and a pension for life? With the exception of a few holdouts, those days are gone and companies who pass out pensions to their employees are about as rare as dinosaur tracks. But the fact of the matter is, people miss the security of their pensions. They liked the idea of knowing exactly how much they were going to receive in the mail each week to pay the bills *and* they liked the security of knowing that it would be there until they died. They want to build a guaranteed income stream that will help them to enjoy retirement and prevent the depletion of their assets in old age. That's the reason why ***income riders*** came along.

I'm not a big fan of variable annuities because you can lose your principal. But variable annuities were the first ones to introduce income riders. They became a part of the fixed annuity world in the mid 2000s. Also known as the GLIB (Guaranteed Lifetime Income Benefit) and the GIB (Guaranteed Income Benefit), and GLWB (Guaranteed Lifetime Withdrawal Benefit), this add-on has become the primary reason why sales of fixed indexed annuities are breaking all records.

LIMRA, the insurance industry market research group, reported in February 2013 that indexed annuity sales for 2012 reached a record high of nearly $34 billion, up 5 percent from 2011 and that 87 percent of indexed annuities sold offer GLWB riders. "When such riders are available, nearly three-quarters of consumers elect them," LIMRA reported, adding that sales of variable annuities were down 7 percent from the previous year.

What that tells me is that more people are interested in guarantees than projections and more concerned about running out of money in retirement than taking one more ride on the stock market roller coaster in search of elusive big gains.

There's no way to accurately convey to you how all the gears work in an FIA with an income rider, but I will give you a broad-brush description. That having been said, however, no question about this useful little tool should go unanswered in any one-on-one appointment made with a competent retirement income specialist.

How Income Riders Work

Think of a fixed indexed annuity with an income rider like a hybrid car that has two engines, one gasoline and one electric. They work differently but each propels the car. The FIA with an income rider has two accounts. One is the surrender value, sometimes called the accumulation account – the amount of money you can walk away with – and the other is there only for the purpose of providing you with an income when you decide it's time to take it. In most cases these two ledgers will have different balances because of the way they work. The income rider balance can increase in value even when the FIA balance is not growing because the index on which its growth is measured is negative. Remember, the "I" in FIA stands for *index.* Its growth is predicated on the growth of the index it is tied to (the S&P 500, for example). What if that index is down? Do you lose your principal? Not in an FIA. Why? Because the "F" stands for *fixed.* You can't lose the money you put in. The worst that can happen is that it will not grow during a negative year but will wait instead until the market moves into positive territory again and pick up from there.

The income rider, however, doesn't work that way. You receive the same level of positive interest in it each and every year, regardless of the movement of the stock market. It is not uncommon for these income riders to accrue at a 7% guaranteed rate. That balance continues growing until you decide to exercise your lifetime income. Then the growth stops and the payout begins. You cannot take the entire income rider value as a lump sum. It must be taken in regular increments.

Let's say you put $500,000 into an FIA and the company gives you a bonus of 8% (this is a common provision), that means that you are starting off with $540,000 in your accumulation account. That same $540,000 will be your starting point for your income account. The insurance industry term for the amount of interest by which the income rider balance increases each year is the "roll-up." Your accumulation account will grow according to the performance of an index, but your income account will get a guaranteed "roll-up" of let's say 7% per year. This will vary from company to company, but the idea is the same. If you had $540,000 to work with, and that income base rolls up at 7 percent per year, then at the end of 10 years you will have an income base of $1,062,262. Can you walk away with that money? No. That's not what it is there for. But what you *can* do is turn on your income and let it continue for the rest of your life (maybe even the life of your spouse, depending on how you structure it when you start it). The income is based on your age. If you are age 75, for example, your payout may be 6.5 percent, or $69,047 per year. Less if you are younger and more if you are older. The idea is to let it grow as long as possible. Use other assets for income if you can while this account has time to ripen and bear fruit, if you will.

Wait a minute! You mean that if I collect this income for 20 years I am going to get $1,380,940 when I only put in $500,000? Yes.

But what happens if you die early? Does the insurance company get to keep my money like it was with the old-style annuities? No. You are not turning your money into a pension. If you were to die tragically in a car accident, for example, the money in your account would be passed along to your heirs. In some cases, the higher income account value can also be used as a death benefit for heirs. It depends on the company and what type of income/death benefit rider you purchase. With today's new age "hybrid" annuities, you do not have to annuitize to get guaranteed-for- life income. That's a huge benefit, and has changed the way income planning can be approached. Not only can you guarantee income, but you are also guaranteed control of your money!

That's an important point to remember because in an immediate annuity, if you put the money in and get a payout for life, your heirs get nothing when you die. FIAs with income riders are very "heir-friendly." Some of them even have additional provisions to cover nursing home stays.

Things you need to know:

- Income riders aren't free. They are paid for by your account. The fee is usually a few basis points (less than one percent) per year. If you aren't interested in turning this bucket of money into an income stream at some point in the future, this is not worth the cost. But if you (a) just aren't sure, or (b) know that you will, it probably is.
- Since your age plays a part in how much you are able to draw from your income rider, you may be too young or too old for this to make sense for you. In fact, most FIA contracts have age restrictions to keep someone young from "breaking the bank." The FIA/income rider money-making machine was built for folks who are either in retirement or within 10 years of it.
- Annuities are not like checking and savings accounts. They have many more moving parts. How do you know if they are for you? That's easy. A visit with a competent retirement income specialist who is capable of analyzing your needs, goals, dreams and desires can tell you.

Avoiding Hidden Investment Costs

The investment world is rife with hidden costs. Only after the damage was done did the captain of the Costa Concordia discover to his horror that he had sailed into concealed danger. Likewise, some investors are oblivious to the danger of hidden investment costs in the form of fees and charges they don't know exist. We already touched on the hidden fees of mutual funds in an earlier chapter, and some have asked how, since they are so egregious, the mutual fund people can still get away with it. The answer is because the lack of transparency required. There is a difference between institutional investing, or wholesale investing, and retail investing.

With mutual funds, you can't see the hidden fees (unless you know just where to look), and because all the money is invested in one large pot, you can't see exactly what you own. Institutional investors who handle large sums of money for corporations hate not knowing exactly where the money is. Larger investors shy away from mutual funds for that reason. A study conducted by the Journal of Financial Planning found people with smaller portfolios (less than $1 million) had more than 80 percent of the money in mutual funds. Those with larger portfolios (more than $1Million) had the exact opposite ratio. In other words only 20 percent was in mutual funds and the rest were in other areas of the investment world. The reason? Hidden fees and lack of transparency. But mutual funds aren't the only investments that have costs. Every investment has costs. Variable annuities have costs.

The example of one couple stands out in my mind. They came to my office for an analysis of their investments, and as it turns out they had $563,000 invested in various accounts.

"How much do you think you are paying in the way of costs?" I asked them after looking over their statements.

"Our advisor tells us that it is about one percent a year in costs," the wife replied.

"Have you ever had an objective third party company evaluate your investments from a standpoint of fees and costs," I asked.

"No. We've never had that done." (I knew they hadn't.)

"Would you like for us to do that for you? It doesn't cost anything," I told them. They agreed.

This couple was paying a total of $16,468 each year in fees and charges. This is not unusual. I have had the same conversation with hundreds of investors over the years. When I asked the couple how much the portfolio was worth 10 years ago, they told me it was worth about the same as it was today. Again, this is not unusual. The last decade has not been all that friendly to undiversified market investors.

What that meant for them, however, was strikingly obvious after the math had a few minutes to sink in. Their money managers had collected $164,580 from the account in the last 10 years. The management fees and account charges were paid from their account to the managers whether the account grew or not! The couple, now entering retirement, had earned virtually nothing in the last 10 years and the handlers of their accounts had earned over $160,000.

The reason why I call these fees and charges "hidden" is because they are just like those rocks in the Mediterranean Sea. They are submerged and hard to find. They don't show up on any bill the account holder's get. You will rarely find them in bold print on the front page of the statement. You may find them in the prospectus, or buried in the fine print, not as a line item, but as a percentage. What you won't *ever* see is:

Fee: $16,468

We should be more concerned about value than we are about cost. Let's say that this same couple who spent this $164,580 in charges and fees in the past 10 years had seen their investment account grow from $500,000 to $1.5 million. What then? Would that $164,580 have been well spent? Of course!

The Ticking IRA Time Bomb

All right, how do you feel about this account?
- Every dollar you withdraw will be taxed
- Distributions can be taxed twice because they often make more of your Social Security income taxable.
- It's the only asset you own that requires you to take distributions whether you want to or not.

When you put it that way, it sort of puts IRAs in a different light, doesn't it? When you are working, you are putting money into a

401(k) or 403(b) or some other tax deferred retirement account. During your working years, that is a great tax shelter, isn't it. Money put away for the future is money you do not pay taxes on that day. It is *deferred*, which means put off until a later date. The money you save is a *deduction* and those are good, right?

Hopefully the money grows. As it grows, you *still* don't pay taxes on it, do you? Do you ever pay taxes on this money at all? Yes. Big time. When you pull it out. Yes, this beautiful tax shelter while you're working suddenly turns into the absolute worst account you can own when you retire. Why? First, when it is all distributions, you are taxed at your highest tax rate, whatever that is. Second, the distributions can be just enough to make at least a portion of your Social Security taxable. Thirdly, you are forced to take out money from this account when you reach age 70 ½ whether you need the money or want the money or not. I am not aware of another type of account that works that way. Finally, from a tax perspective, if you leave this account to your spouse or heirs, you have instantly saddled them with a huge tax burden and in many cases the lion's share of the asset ends up in Uncle Sam's coffers.

Think about this. When a husband and wife file jointly, you have two standard tax deductions and two personal exemptions, and you have a better tax rate. But what happens when one of them passes away? Now the surviving spouse has one standard deduction, one personal exemption, and their tax rates go up. This individual now earns less and pays more in taxes.

Not only that, but these accounts are *completely* exposed to future tax increases. I love to take an informal survey when I speak to a group and ask them whether they think taxes will (a) go down in the future, (b) go up in the future, or (c) remain about the same. Every hand goes up for (b) – go up in the future. Then I like to poll the group and ask if they think that taxes will only go up for the rich, or if they think all of us will end up paying more in taxes. The vote is always for the latter.

Taxes are one of the most important concerns when deciding on an investment. Take the case of a married couple, each 65 years old. They have an IRA worth $500,000. Let's assume they earn 6 percent over time. Let's also assume that one of them lives to age 90. That means that if all they take out of the account is their RMD (Required Minimum Distribution) they will end up paying tax on $900,000 before they die. Are they through paying taxes? Yes, ***they*** are because they're dead. But there is more taxes to be paid. There is still $700,000 left in the account. Who gets that? The heirs. Usually the kids.

Stretching the IRA is one way of keeping the account growing and reducing the immediate tax burden. But the heirs also inherit the RMD. The percentage they are required to withdraw, since it is based on their age and the government's life expectancy tables, will increase as they grow older. By pulling out the minimum, however, they are able to enjoy that money for years to come and even pass it on to the next generation. But assuming the 6 percent growth factor, when it is all said and done, the IRS will collect taxes on $1.6 million.

Some may have wondered what Uncle Sam was thinking when he allowed us way back when to put that money aside without having taxes come out of our paycheck. Uncle Sam was pretty smart when you stop and think about it.

Let's say you are a farmer. You are growing corn. You walk into your favorite feed and seed store to buy seed for your spring planting season. You spot a fellow over near the cash register. He has a star-spangled top hat and is sporting a long, gray pointy beard. It's good old Uncle Sam!

"I'll make you a deal," he says.

"I'm all ears," you say (pardon the pun).

"You can go ahead and pay me tax on the seed right now and be done with it, or you can wait until you harvest the corn and pay me tax on all you harvest."

Of course you would pay the tax and be done with it! Who wouldn't?

Good question. Apparently the millions and millions of Americans who salt their money away in tax deferred status, waiting for it to grow into nice, big fat accounts, when they will pay (probably) higher tax rates on more money.

Back to our 65-year-old couple with the $500,000 IRA for a moment. What if someone could have reached out to them and told them way back then that there were ways they could still grow their account to 1.6 million dollars and not have to fork over $500,000 to the IRS? What if there was a way to tell them that their tax obligation may be only a third of that? Do you think they would be interested in a strategy that would accomplish that? A Roth conversion is one of them. Roth conversion of an IRA isn't for everyone, and it may not work for you. But it is worth looking into if you have an IRA and you haven't checked it out.

What amazes me is how few financial advisors are having conversations with their clients about strategies to minimize taxes. There are three areas where every red-blooded, tax-paying, IRA-owning member of the American investing public should be totally informed and thoroughly educated but are not:

- Stretch IRAs/Stretch Roth IRAs
- Roth Conversion/Systematic Roth Conversion
- Life Leveraged Plans

Chapter Nine

How Much Liquidity Do You Really Need in Retirement?

There's no doubt about it. People like liquidity. Just the thought of being able to access all of your assets at any time creates the pleasant feeling of control. Remember Scrooge McDuck from the old Donald Duck cartoons? Walt Disney never told us how the old duck got so rich, but in the comic books and films he could be seen diving into his money bin and splashing around in his millions as if it were a swimming pool. That's liquidity!

Exploring the "What ifs" of Liquidity

As we established in Chapter Four, liquidity is great but that warm and fuzzy feeling of being able to access your money at a moment's notice comes with a price tag. Accounts that offer great liquidity provide low rates of return. When it comes to deciding how much of their assets need to be liquid many play the "what if" game. What if I suddenly need cash for an emergency? What if my roof needs replacing? What If the car breaks down? What if this? What if that? The problem is, it's easy to "what if" yourself into a situation where you have too much liquidity. If you have excess liquidity, you run the very real risk of outliving your income. Money that's 100 percent liquid probably isn't working very hard.

"What if I want to buy a new home after I retire?" There's a situation where you will need liquid assets. That's one of those decisions you need to have nailed down before you retire if at all possible. The old conventional wisdom was to pay off your house and retire without a mortgage. But times are changing. An article entitled "7 Reasons Not to Pay Off Your Mortgage Before You Retire" appeared in the January 3, 2014 issue of *Forbes* magazine and put a question mark on that old rule of thumb.

"It might be a better option today to keep paying a monthly mortgage payment in retirement rather than using assets to pay it off," the article said. Keeping your money in an annuity yielding 6 percent while you continue to make monthly payments on a mortgage loan charging 4.5 percent would give you a net gain of 1.5 percent wouldn't it? For the sake of easy math, let's say you have a $100,000 mortgage and you gain $1,500 per year by keeping the mortgage. Compounded at 6 percent that would amount to a whopping $60,000 in 20 years. And, the only thing you had to do to claim that windfall was resist the urge to pay off your mortgage or pay cash for a new house.

"What if I need to purchase a new car?" With people living longer these days, this is a good possibility. Current statistics say that, on average, if you have already lived to be 65 and you are in average health, you have a 47 percent chance of living to be 85, whether you are male or female. Unfortunately the life expectancy of our cars hasn't changed. According to Polk, an automotive data and marketing research organization, the average age of a car on U.S. highways is 11.1 years. So, yes, you will probably need to replace your car once or twice in retirement. And maybe this is one of your personal perks in life. Maybe you enjoy driving newer cars. If so, then this is a good reason to keep the amount of money necessary to facilitate this expense liquid. By liquid, I mean checking, savings, money market accounts - "under the pillow" liquid. Now with liquid you get low rates of return, no tax advantages, no guaranteed income benefits etc. That's the price you pay for total liquidity. The reason I don't consider CDs, bonds, or stock market investments liquid is because CDs have a term attached to them and they can penalize you up to six months of interest (as this is written, that's not going to amount to much). In my opinion, Equities, stocks and bond are only liquid when the investment is rising in value and not when the market tanks! Look at what happened in 2000, 2001, 2002 and 2008. If your account is down 20 or 30 percent in value, how liquid is it? Most folks would not even consider taking money out (unless they have to) because they would lose money and "lock in losses". At that point how liquid are equity investments? It all depends on whether they are up or down, so you be the judge. I'll stand by my reasoning from pure experience, and simple math!

"What if I need to lend money to my children?" We have to get real here. Lending money to our children is a gift. As much as we would like to help them—while they are in their earning years—our first obligation is to our own financial stability. It may not be easy, but ask them to seek other solutions. I once knew a father who was always financing his daughter's car loans. However, after her 30th birthday, he refused. She was a little ticked at him at first, but then she did what she had to do. She went to the bank and secured her own loan. She later thanked him. It gave her confidence and taught her independence and responsibility. Now she knew that she could do this for herself, even if her father was no longer there to lean on.

I realize I am treading on thin ice here. These decisions are, after all, personal. But tough love is sometimes the best kind. Usually I don't care much for television commercials, but I saw one the other day that touched me. The scene opens with a young girl changing a tire in an empty parking lot. She is having trouble loosening the lug nuts. She has to stand up and use her foot on the lug wrench but she eventually gets the job done. You think she is all alone in this lonely, deserted place. Then you see feet coming into the picture around the back of the car. Uh oh, you think. This isn't good. Then the young girl's face looks up and breaks into a big smile. Then you hear the only dialogue in the commercial as the man, who is obviously the girl's father, smiles and says, "I knew you could do it." He was teaching his daughter to change a tire. I couldn't help but think of my daughter, Kelly, even though she is an adult now and part of the office staff at JDS Wealth Management Corp. I think the commercial was produced by an automobile company, but I honestly don't remember. But the moral of the story was tough love. It also left me wondering if Kelly knew how to change a car tire?

If you decide you want to lend money to your children, I invite you to revisit the subheading in Chapter Six—Becoming a Bank for Family Members. You may consider adding predetermined amount to your liquidity fund to cover this contingency. That gives you a limit so you don't become an open checkbook for family members. It allows you to set a limit that is easier to stick to.

"What if a great investment opportunity comes along? Won't I need some liquid funds to take advantage of it?" This one reminds me of people who like to keep large amounts of cash in their wallets. Salespeople seem to have an uncanny ability to sniff out "walking wallets" to entice them with the most amazing array of great deals, new gadgets, or grand opportunities. Before our cash-rich friends know it, their money has jumped out of their wallet and into someone else's. Unfortunately, I've seen the same thing happen to some after they retire. Once you begin viewing your reserves as ready cash there is the temptation to dip into them. The problem with investing with large sums of money after you retire is that any losses you may incur come with dearer consequences. You are using assets that are probably to some degree non-renewable resources and time is not on your side when it comes to recouping those losses. Also, keeping very large amounts of liquid assets available for "the chance of a lifetime" investment can lead to an emotional decision. I once knew of an individual who invested $100,000 in a golf course that he just knew couldn't lose. What is it worth today? Zero. I can't help but think that if the money had been more difficult to access, he probably wouldn't have made such a foolish decision.

Health—Four Issues to Consider

As the old Geritol commercial says, "If you've got your health, you've got just about everything." Conversely, when your health is threatened, it becomes your number one priority. Essentially we need to look at four health issues: Health Care / Medicare, uncovered prescriptions, long term care, and death.

Let's tackle death first. Yes, you will need cash available immediately following your demise. But instead of reserving an inordinate amount of cash to be available at a time when heirs are least emotionally ready to make sound decisions, why not do a little planning instead? A client of mine recently told me that one of the greatest gifts that his mother ever gave him was her pre-planned funeral. Her death came at a time when he was going through what he called a "rough patch." His life was in a veritable shambles from both a personal and professional standpoint. And then, when he could least handle another trauma, his mother died. But she had possessed the foresight to prepare everything in advance. She had selected the church, the cemetery plot, the headstone, all of which was paid for. She had even written down the songs she wanted sung at her funeral service, the pall bearers, the flowers, the dress in which she wished to be buried. All he had to do was follow the script. He knew that his mother would have been pleased and that was comforting to him.

It makes sense to plan and prepay final arrangements. I know of one man who lived well into his 80s and loved baseball. He wanted his funeral to be a fun time. He wanted no dirges or hymns at his funeral. He requested that everyone join in singing the old baseball standard, "Take Me Out To the Ball Game." He even had copies of the sheet music for the 1908 classic printed up with his personal instructions as to when and how he wanted it sung. This man helped his family celebrate his life with joy—something they may not have had the courage to do had he not preplanned and prepaid his "going away party."

Prescriptions not covered by insurance can be a costly affair when you are on a fixed income. My advice is first to make sure you are doing all you can through Medicare. Go to the Medicare website, www.Medicare.gov , and read online or download the free booklet *Medicare & You*, which is a comprehensive reference guide published each year by the Centers for Medicare & Medicaid Services. Specifically, you are going to be interested in Part D for prescription drugs. Part D has solved much of the prescription drug dilemma, but because the government privatized this portion of Medicare, there are currently more than 1,000 Part D plans to choose from. Once you do your homework, it will be easier to plan for the coverage that you need beyond Medicare.

Long term care is a genuine concern. As we mentioned earlier in this book, the statistics are that an average couple age 65 faces a 70 percent chance that one of them will require long term health care. Who is going to pay for it?

The first myth to debunk is that Medicare is going to take care of this for you. In a nutshell, Medicare won't cover the cost of nursing homes or assisted living facilities. See the details in the Medicare booklet *Medicare & You* which available free of charge online at www.medicare.gov.

So what are your other options? One solution is to purchase long term health care insurance. However, as you might have guessed, this insurance is most affordable when you are least likely to need it—ages 40-55. And, it is most costly when you are most likely to need it—after 65. In fact, by the time you are age 65, it may be too costly or you may no longer qualify. More importantly, it operates like car insurance. Premiums can go up even if you have owned the policy for several years. In fact, you need to **expect** premiums to increase. According to the *Kiplinger* report entitled, "What to Do When Your Long-term Health Care Rates Go Up," policyholders need to expect a 20% to 30% rate increase every five years. On the bright side, most insurance companies will let you reduce your benefits or lower your built-in inflation protection as a way to lower your premium. Like car insurance, long term health care premiums are not returned if you don't use it, unless of course you've purchased that expensive "return of premium" rider.

Asset-based Long Term Care, A New Age Planning Tool

The "use-it-or-lose it" aspect of traditional long-term care insurance has never set well with the baby boom generation. So a few years ago, insurance companies designed some new **"hybrid"** options. Let's face it...insurance companies are in business to make a profit, and they have to make their products appealing. There was a time when long term care insurance was affordable and the terms of the policies were reasonable. But we have seen that change since the 1970s when they were first introduced. What happened? For one thing, government regulations forced LTC facilities to improve their level of care. These facilities, of course, passed the increased costs along to the public. Premiums for insurance went up as a result and carriers found it more difficult to market the insurance. Many carriers decided to just leave the LTC market. Insurance companies began looking for ways to retool their approach to LTC and they have come up with some interesting solutions.

Combos – These are hybrid, or combination policies. They combine long term care benefits with life insurance or annuities. One of these new contracts that is gaining in popularity combines aspects of the traditional fixed annuity with traditional LTC. The fixed annuity side of the contract offers a guaranteed interest rate that is typically more than double what a bank CD would pay and the LTC side of the contract pays out two to three times the annuity value over two, four, or up to six years. Let's say that someone deposited $100,000 into one of these instruments. They might have a benefit limit of 300 percent (in other words, a ceiling of $300,000 in LTC benefits). The initial

$100,000 would be spent first, followed by an additional $200,000, or up to that amount. When the money runs out the benefits end. When the time of coverage runs out the benefits end.

What if you buy one of these combined policies and you never need long-term care? Then the product acts just like any other traditional fixed annuity. The value of the annuity can be passed on to heirs upon your death. Most carriers require at least $50,000 - $100,000 up front deposit. This is a general description of the concept. The terms of the contract vary from carrier to carrier. One more advantage to these new combination policies comes from the government. The Pension Protection Act of 2006 created a provision making premiums paid for LTC insurance tax free if they are paid from an annuity.

This new approach solves a problem, but these products are not for everybody. I recommend that you see a competent retirement planning specialist who is current on these contracts so you can see if they are suitable for you. There may be some underwriting involved because of the LTC portion of the contract so health issues may disqualify you. Just how strict those underwriting guidelines are will vary from carrier to carrier.

These are much more appealing than the use-it-or-lose-it traditional LTC policies, especially for persons who are approaching retirement and have enough in the way of assets to invest.

Life Insurance/LTC Combos - Life insurance has morphed and changed over the years at an alarming rate. Why? Because insurance companies have realized that people are living longer, and baby boomers (78 million of us) are going to need more strategic ways to plan for long term care and taxes. This allows them to receive or control premium for longer periods of time before they have to pay claims. Therefore, premiums have dropped drastically over the years!

These newer "hybrid" life insurance / LTC combos provide folks with tremendous leverage of their dollars, assuming they are insurable. Let's look at a few examples to make it simple. These programs can either be purchased as a single premium, or 10-pay, or annual premium for life.

Male age 60 - $100,000 single premium, rated at preferred non-tobacco.

This buys a $250,000 guaranteed death benefit, with a return of premium rider included. The ROP rider guarantees the $100,000 premium can never be lost, but can grow. It's also 100 percent liquid after the first year. For LTC benefits, 74 percent of the death benefit can be used for LTC, paid out monthly over six years ($250,000 x 74 percent = $185,000 at $2,569 per month).

Any money not used, is passed on to heirs *income tax free!*

What a great way to gain leverage against an insurance company!!

Male age 67 – Annual premium of $10,000 rated at preferred non-tobacco. This buys a $500,000 guaranteed death benefit with LTC benefits the same as above ($500,000 x 74 percent = $370,000 at $5,138 per month).

The bottom line is this: These strategies provide tremendous leverage using life insurance for income replacement, legacy planning, tax planning, and long term care planning all in one policy. Someone will always benefit from this type of strategy. That's why we call it "hybrid."

Not All Policies Are the Same

Just as not all insurance companies are the same, not all combination / hybrid policies are the same. I suggest you do your due diligence before buying one. Check the company ratings. Something you need to understand about insurance company ratings is this: Ratings organizations, such as A.M. Best, Moody's, and Standard and Poors merely evaluate and rate the insurance company's financial soundness. There are other factors that which will enter into your decision, such as the company's willingness and capacity to handle claims properly and the quality of the company's customer service. Extremely important are such things as "legal reserves", or how much money the insurance company has in reserve to back all policyholders. Most of the companies we work with have approximately $1.05 - $1.08 in reserve for every dollar on deposit. Risk-based capital is also important. My point is, there are other things just as important to the insurance company's stability as ratings.

When you do a benefits/premium analysis you will find there are significant differences. The American Association for Long Term Care Insurance looked at two policies from two top rated insurance companies and compared them. They ran an illustration using a married female, age 62 and a single premium deposit of $100,000. Notice the difference:

Policy A would pay a Death Benefit of **$193,906** and a monthly long term care benefit of **$8,079.**

Policy B would pay a Death Benefit of **$150,121** and a monthly long term care benefit of **$6,255.**

Policy C would pay a Death Benefit of **$165,997** and a monthly long term care benefit of **$5,533.**

A Few Asset Based Long Term Care Examples

Let's take a look at the "asset based long term care" strategy that was mentioned earlier, and is becoming very popular with planners and baby boomers alike. This is a single-premium policy like the one shown above. It provides tax free life insurance, return of premium after the second year, a guarantee of premium at all times and outstanding leverage for long term care. It stands to reason that the older you are, the less your benefits will be. Here's a recent case:

Male age 60 – $100,000 single premium, rated at standard non-tobacco, with return of premium rider included. In this case, $100,000 buys a $213,015 of guaranteed tax-free death benefit. The premium is 100 percent liquid after year two. The long term care benefit is $573,876, paid out at $7,971 per month for six years. What a tremendous way to leverage money against an insurance company in case of unforeseen health issues. Keep in mind, you must be insurable. Here are the benefits in menu form

1) Premium is 100 percent liquid and protected after year two.
2) The death benefit more than doubles your money immediately, and is tax free to heirs.
3) The long term care benefit is huge considering money invested, especially since the premium is always liquid if you need it.

Of course, if you pull out premium, you lose your benefits. But that's a choice you can always make. The long term care benefit is also intended to pay out income tax free. What more can you ask for? Someone always wins with this strategy, not just the big bad insurance company.

The benefit/premium picture is not the only criteria but it is probably the most important. This is one of those areas where you may find it prudent to consult a professional who understands how these "hybrid" products function, and can make sure that you get the best coverage for your premium dollar. Oh! By the way - our number at JDS Wealth Management Corp. is 704-660-0214 (do I need to apologize for that shameless plug)?

Avoid Procrastination

Most modern sailing vessels have an arrangement of stanchions and cables around the perimeter of their decks designed to keep you from falling overboard if you stumble. Appropriately, these cables are called "lifelines." By design, these barriers are light-weight and unobtrusive so as not to interfere with the performance of the boat or your sailing experience. One of the cardinal safety rules of moving about on the deck of a sailboat is:"Always keep one hand for the boat." Essentially it means to plan your steps carefully so there is always a hand-hold nearby. The ocean is fickle and a sudden gust of wind or a wave can cause you to lose your balance. The lifeline, of course, is there to prevent you from slipping overboard at last resort.

Another safety rule when getting on or off a sail boat is to step purposely onto the boat from the dock or purposely onto the dock from the boat. Whatever you do, don't step indecisively and leave one foot on the boat and one foot on the dock. Why is this a recipe for disaster? The boat may drift away from the dock with you half on and half off and your next destination will likely be in the water. When leaving the dock, get both feet on the vessel side of the lifeline as quickly as possible.

I've seen the same thing happen when people make decisions about liquidity. At this transition point, new retirees can sometimes straddle the fence, keeping too much of their portfolio liquid for too long. The real blow comes when it becomes apparent that their assets will not last throughout their full retirement. If the decision about liquidity is a tough one for you, consult a financial advisor who specializes in retirement income planning. Once you are comfortable with the plan and confident it fits your unique financial situation, stick to it. Liquidity is like that lifeline. It's there for emergencies but it is better not to have to rely on it. It's a good thing – there to protect you – but don't trip over it.

Chapter Ten

Taking a Fresh Look at Life Insurance and Annuities

You have to go back to the days of the Romans to find the roots of life insurance. In 100 B.C. Roman soldiers knew that when they went into battle there would be a good chance they would never make it home. But the pay was good and there was a degree of prestige in being one of the best professional soldiers the world had ever known.

Roman soldiers also insisted on being buried with their ancestors if at all possible. Why? Because if they weren't they would be tortured in the afterlife. At least that is what they believed. Despite the dangers of hacking swords with and hurling spears at the Huns and Barbarians, more soldiers survived the Roman wars than died in them. However, to ensure they would have a decent burial if the worst happened to them, the soldiers pooled their money into a fund that would be used to lay to rest the ones who died in battle, burying them with their ancestors so as not to anger the gods. It was the first time in recorded history that the concept of creating a risk pool was used to offset cost.

Eventually the idea of burial insurance gained a footing with the general population. And then, in 476 A.D., when Rome fell, insurance disappeared about as abruptly as it first appeared on the world scene. It wouldn't be until 1662, almost 1200 years later, that a curious Englishman named John Graunt would resurrect interest in life insurance. Although he was a draper by trade, Graunt was intrigued by the *Bills of Mortality*—a published list of deaths spanning 70 years. By studying the documents, Graunt was able to predict the percentage of people who would survive to each successive age and the life expectancies of various groups of people. Armed with reliable statistics, life insurance companies began to emerge in England as early as 1706. It would take another 50 years or so for life insurance to make its way across the ocean to America. In 1776, America won her independence and the British were sent home. Life insurance, however, stayed and became a fixture of American economic life. Today, there are more than 1,200 life and health insurance companies in the U.S.

Traditional Role of Life Insurance

Life insurance has changed since the days of Ancient Rome. It does a lot more than pay for burial expenses. According to the 2013 Insurance Barometer Study, over 70 percent of retirees age 65 and older own life insurance. Why? Take a look at the list below.

- ***Providing for Loved Ones*** - Few things bring greater peace of mind than knowing that our loved ones will be cared for even when we are gone. In fact, according to the 2013 Insurance Barometer Study, the loss of a relative or close friend—whether they had insurance or not—proved to be the top motivator for people to shop and likely make sure their own insurance was in order.
- ***Personal Debt Payment*** - No one wants to leave a mess behind. Life insurance is a reliable way to settle our personal debts upon our demise. The *Time* Magazine article "Americans Are Taking on Debt at Scary High Rates" published February 19, 2014, stated that auto loans, student loans, and credit card debt all increased in the last quarter of 2013. Putting that in perspective, in 2013 the average auto loan balance in the U.S. was about $15,000, average student loan balance was $29,000, and the average credit card debt was $7123. People purchase polices to insure that their debts are cleaned up.
- ***Funeral Expenses*** - The average funeral costs about $6,600, with an additional expense of up to $3,000 for the gravesite, vault, or liner. However, caskets alone can cost up to $10,000 and often grieving family members make emotional purchases that later rob them of life insurance intended for their support. Reading the *Fox Business* newsletter titled "10 Facts Funeral Directors May Not Tell You" should be enough to motivate

you to go ahead and plan your funeral and pay for it in advance as we discussed in the last chapter.
- *Mortgage Debt*- It is a good feeling to know that your significant other will not have to worry about a house payment if you die prematurely. Mortgage insurance can be purchased directly from the mortgage company or independently. In either case, it is usually a decreasing term policy that expires with the term of the mortgage. The average mortgage balance is $150,000.
- *Planned Giving*- Favorite churches, universities, or other charities can be named as beneficiaries on life insurance policies purchased specifically to fund a gift. This is also a great way to create a legacy for our heirs.
- *College Funds*- Parents or grandparents often earmark life insurance policies for the specific purpose of paying for college expenses for children. The website, www.collegedata.com, reported, "In its most recent survey of college pricing, the College Board reports that a "moderate" college budget for an in-state public college for the 2013–2014 academic year averaged $22,826. A moderate budget at a private college averaged $44,750."
- *Taxes*- Having immediate and sufficient funds—such as the proceeds from life insurance—can pay for federal estate taxes and state inheritance taxes which can preserve the value of your estate. Do you have an IRA, 401(k) or other pre-tax qualified retirement plan? What do you think happens to the money when it passes on to someone other than your spouse? Yeah, you guessed it! It is all taxed! So, life insurance is often used to replace taxes on IRAs and preserve wealth for loved ones.
- *Income Replacement* – Folks who fail to plan don't consider what happens when a spouse passes away. In almost all cases, one thing is for sure – *income is lost.* Social Security, pensions, income from work…just to name a few. When you think about all the ways income could be lost at the passing of a loved one it becomes very clear how a tax free life insurance policy can replace that lost income. This type of insurance should be called *love* insurance, not *life* insurance!

Advantages of Life Insurance for Retirement Planning

In the past, life insurance benefits were pigeon holed as money that the insured would never see. Instead, death benefits would be paid to your named beneficiary. Just glance through the list above and you will see that your family, your funeral home, your mortgage company, or somebody other than you got the check from the insurance company. Well, that was then and this is now.

Today, investment grade insurance policies are designed so that you benefit from the policy while you are still alive. These investment grade policies originated in the late 1970s. They allow investors to accumulate **tax-advantaged retirement funds**. In fact, these new policies became so popular that new laws were put in place in the 1980s to prevent the tax benefits of life insurance from being abused. The first law, TEFRA, is an acronym for *Tax, Equity, Fiscal and Responsibility Act of 1982*. The next law, DEFRA stands for *Deficient Reduction Act of 1984* and the final law, TAMRA is expanded to *Technical and Miscellaneous Revenue Act of 1988*. Again, these laws regulate "investment grade life insurance."

Question: What Is Investment Grade Life Insurance?
Answer: A tax-free retirement!

Let's start with a quick review of traditional life insurance. Term is the least expensive and simplest form of insurance. It is known as "pure risk protection" because term insurance does not accumulate any cash value. Similar to your homeowner's policy, term insurance only pays if you have a claim. As the name implies, term insurance protects you for a predetermined length of time, usually 10-20 years. When the contract expires, if you wish to purchase a new term policy, your new rate will be based on your current age, current health or insurability, and the number of years that you specify.

Permanent insurance commonly known as whole life costs more initially but is usually less expensive over the course of a lifetime. This is due to the fact that once you sign the contract, your premium and death benefit are locked in for the rest of your life—regardless of age or insurability—as long as you pay the premiums. A second advantage of permanent insurance is that cash value accumulates. The cash value can then be used to pay premiums when times get lean or to save for retirement. Both term and permanent insurance pay death benefits to the named beneficiary in exchange for premium payments.

Investment grade insurance didn't arrive on the world scene until the late 1970s. It is a type of **permanent** insurance, but it satisfies the boomer generations demand for higher growth potential. Probably, had the boomers not made a stink about the low rates insurance companies paid on whole life cash values this new plan may never have come into existence. But as my mom, Doris Stillman, used to remind me, "Necessity is the mother of invention." The necessity that created this change occurred when interest rates soared to over 15 percent in the early 1980s. Boomers looked in dismay as their insurance companies pretended that nothing had changed and continued to pay a miserly 3 or 4 percent on cash values. Without much conversation, the boomers took action. In record numbers, they cashed in their whole life policies, bought term insurance, and invested the difference in the bank where money markets and CDs were paying 12 percent or more. Alarmed by the mass exodus and perhaps embracing the motto that "the customer is always right," insurance companies developed a new policy that met the demands of this savvy new generation. This new generation of permanent life insurance paid interest based on U.S. Treasury Bills and openly disclosed all fees, charges, and mortality costs. It was also given a new name—**Universal Life**, nicknamed **UL**.

Universal Life appealed to the baby boomers because it puts everything back in one place and it brings the growth back under the tax-deferred umbrella. As with traditional insurance, you pay premiums, but with UL the premiums are flexible. This allows you to invest more when times are prosperous so that you have more money working towards your retirement in a tax-deferred vehicle. Withdrawals are flexible too. Policy owners have the freedom to take low interest loans at no penalty as they see fit. At the same time, as with all life insurance, the benefits are paid to the named beneficiaries **tax free.**

Boomers seemed to be pretty pleased with this new UL policy until the stock market took off. This could have meant trouble for the insurance companies again. However, this time, the insurance companies were quick to notice public sentiment to ditch the slower moving UL policies for a stock portfolio. They created the new **Indexed Universal Life (IUL)** before a stampede ensued. Voting with their pocketbooks, the boomers liked IUL and for good reason. This policy had a built in ratchet that let them get the best of both worlds. In other words, when the market moves up, cash values go up based on the stock market index. But when the market goes down, their cash values were locked in and preserved.

Retirement Advantages of IUL Policies

- **Guaranteed principal and gains**— Retirees in IUL policies benefited from the stock market growth in the 2000s, but they did not lose any principal or gains in the 2008 crisis. Let me repeat that. *Investors in IUL polices did not lose any principal or gains in the 2008 stock market crash!*
- **Opportunity for higher returns**— Because the increase in cash value is based on a stock market index, instead of U.S. Treasury Bills, investors have the opportunity for substantial gains. Investors also keep their gains, even in a falling market, thanks to the ratchet feature.
- **Tax-free cash flow in retirement**— Through the use of contract loans investors can create a stream of income during retirement that is free of federal, state, local, AND the alternative minimum tax.
- **Heirs receive a tax-free death benefit**— The check that your named beneficiary receives from your IUL policy will be just like any other death benefit. It will be tax free.

Universal Variable Life - Variable life policies invest the cash value in the stock market through "Sub Accounts" much like variable annuities. So, the opportunity for growth of the cash value is much greater but so is the opportunity for loss. I've seen variable life policies crash and burn in market downturns such as 2000-2002, and 2008. So these policies must be monitored very carefully. I'll admit, I'm not a big fan of these types of policies. Especially since the new "hybrid" indexed UL's have come of age.

A Few Caveats

IUL's are long term investments. Aside from taking into consideration your age, health, and the other pieces to your retirement puzzle, insist that your retirement advisor walk you through each of these design features of IULs.

- By design, IULs are intended to be held for a minimum 10-15 years. Know the cost for cancellation or early surrender fees prior to investing.
- The mortality cost is disclosed and deducted from the contract value. Know how the actual insurance cost will affect the net return
- Realize that the issuing company can change the policy rates and fees annually as they deem necessary.
- Understand the impact of a policy lapse. This can trigger a taxable event.

How about Safety?

I have to chuckle when people call in to my Radio show (WSIC 1400 AM) to ask me if life insurance or annuities are insured by FDIC. The callers often know that FDIC is an acronym for Federal Deposit Insurance Corporation. But what they don't realize is that this is an insurance company. It was set in place by Congress to insure bank deposits. But that raises the question: Who insures insurance companies? Really, when you think about it, would it make any sense for one insurance company to insure another? The answer is a resounding YES! This is called "reinsurance." All insurance is based on the concept of "pooled money". In other words, a whole bunch of people pay premiums into a "pool" of money that only a few people use. So, collectively these insurance companies have tremendous assets in reserve (explained below).

The insurance industry figured out that they could use their "pooled" assets to back each other up if needed. In other word, "you wash my back, and I'll wash yours." This "reinsurance" strategy provides unparalleled safety for consumers using "legal reserve insurance companies".

The federal government came up with another solution to "insure" the safety of insurance companies and it is a very good solution in my opinion. The law requires insurance companies to set aside reserves equal to 100 percent of their liabilities. Hence, the phrase that you will often see on insurance companies' websites and in their printed literature is **"100 percent legal reserve insurance company."** In addition to this, the government regulates how those reserved assets are invested. In reality, most legal reserve insurance companies have approximately $1.04 - $1.08 in reserve for every dollar on deposit. Folks, that's awesome protection during economic hard times! There could never be a run on a legal reserve insurance company like a bank, investment bank, or brokerage firm (exactly what happened to Wachovia, Leman Brothers, Bear Stearns, Merrill Lynch, etc., because they had most of the their money *leveraged* and not accessible when customers came calling). Because the insurance company has more money in reserve and liquid then would ever be required to pay off all current policyholders, a run on a legal reserve insurance company is never a concern. Looking at their history, insurance companies have a remarkable record of safety and solvency.

A New Look At Annuities

Last year, Americans invested a record $33.9 billion in fixed index annuities, according to a 2013 report by LIMRA, a worldwide research institute. Surprised? Well, these new annuities, just like the new life insurance policies are not the investment vehicles that your daddy drove around. These are designed to meet the performance demands of the new and savvy boomer generation.

But first, let's do a brief recap on the "old model" annuities. You deposit a lump sum with the insurer and your money will grow tax deferred at a fixed rate of return and a guaranteed return of principal. At retirement, you either choose monthly checks for life or monthly checks for a set number of years. If you choose the paychecks for life—you have the peace of mind that you can live to be as old as Methuselah (the oldest living man according to the Bible at 969 years), and you will get a check for exactly the same amount every month until you draw your last breath. On the downside though, if you die early your heirs don't see a dime. It all gets folded back into the annuity pool to spread the risk/reward over a large group of annuity owners.

As you might guess, the boom generation didn't like this idea for a couple of reasons. Number one, they didn't want the insurance company or even fellow annuity owners ending up with what they deemed was their rightful inheritance. A close second to this complaint was the realization that traditional annuities grew at a very low fixed rate. So, insurance companies developed the kind of annuity vehicle that boomers could really get behind.

Hybrid / Fixed Index Annuities

Fixed index annuities retain all the benefits of annuities with the addition of some extra features. Listed are features shared by all annuities:

- All annuities are issued by insurance companies
- Annuity benefits avoid probate and are passed to heirs immediately upon the death of the owner
- Earnings grow tax deferred and are taxed as ordinary income when withdrawn
- Principal is guaranteed by the issuer on all FIXED annuities

The first modification made to this new generation of annuities is hinted at in its name—fixed index. Instead of paying a flat rate of return on your cash value, insurance companies link your returns to a stock index fund such as the S&P 500. Your investment can grow to a predetermined capped limit of 6-10 percent in a favorable market. This cap might seem a little conservative, but here is the tradeoff. In a falling market, you retain ALL of your gains and NEVER LOSE PRINCIPAL. This was a huge plus for my clients in 2008. I almost had T-shirts printed that said "My retirement plan didn't lose a dime in the 2008," but decided against the idea because too many people were hurting. Oh, aside from the great potential for growth, remember that the growth in fixed income annuities is all tax deferred until you withdraw funds. Then, the funds are taxed as ordinary income.

Another modification centers on the fees. Boomers didn't want fees in this new investment vehicle, especially hidden fees. Believe it or not, they got what they wanted. There are no hidden fees, no investment fees, no maintenance fees, simply no fees. Of course, if you add on extras such as an income rider, then you will pay for that. But we will discuss that in a minute.

The final modification addressed the death benefit. Remember how it irked the boomers that the standard annuities pay no death benefit—even if you die only two years after purchasing the policy? Well, in the fixed index annuity, heirs inherit any unspent balance. It is free of probate, but they will have to pay taxes on it. But at least the rightful heirs are getting an inheritance.

Income Riders, A Hybrid Option

When you couple an income rider with a fixed indexed annuity you create an "income annuity" or "hybrid annuity." This adds flexibility to your fixed income annuity by giving you access to your account balance without disrupting your guaranteed lifetime income.

Remember the LIMRA report that we talked under the subheading, "A New Look At Annuities?" It said the Americans invested a record $33.9 billion in fixed index annuities in 2013. That is great for the investor because supply and demand has caused insurance companies to sweeten the deal for investors who add on the income rider. Currently, many issuers are offering a cash bonus of up to 8 percent. (Note: In some cases it could be as high as 10-12 percent but you'll have to call me to learn about that) So if you deposit $275,000, the insurer immediately credits an additional $22,000 to your account. That means that your account value begins at $297,000.

To accomplish all the objectives in the hybrid income annuity—higher returns, death benefits, and low fees—the insurer actually sets up two accounts in your contract. For accounting purposes, you will have an **accumulation account** and an **income account**. The balance in each account begins at $297,000. The **accumulation account** is linked to a stock market index that has various indexing strategies. Caps, participation rates, and spreads are applied that will limit upside potential gains. But, the silver lining is that your downside is always limited to zero percent ; you can never lose money due to a stock market reversal. You get upside potential, with no downside risk? Not a bad tradeoff in my opinion, ***especially in retirement when risk needs to be reduced.*** Additionally, many carriers build in a floor of 1.25

percent guaranteeing that even in a losing stock market, your account will experience some growth.

Gains are usually locked in annually, and can't be lost once credited. This is known as an "annual reset and ratchet". Projecting this out at a 6 percent rate of return (approximately what fixed indexed annuities have averaged since their inception in 1995), your **accumulation account** would be valued at $531,882. On the flipside, if the market plummeted the entire 10 years, the built in floor would support your account, giving you an actual account value of $336,284. That is pretty amazing when you compare it to what happened to most people in 2000, 2001, 2002 and 2008 who were in the stock market.

Moving on to the **income account,** again you begin with $297,000. This time however, your account is linked to a stated rate that generally hovers around a 7-8 percent guaranteed minimum for up to 20 years. Calculating this for the same 10-year period, your **income account** will be valued at $584,244. Now it's time to launch your income rider.

In a typical example—every carrier has its own formula—if you decide to start collecting checks at age 65, your payout will be 5.5 percent of your **income account** or $32,133 per year for the rest of your life. If you wait until you are 75 to collect your checks, your annual payout goes up to 6.5 percent or $37,976. Now, just to have a little fun with "possibility thinking," if you live to be 95, you would actually collect $759,520 and you only put in $275,000 when you started. And, think about this – what if you had started collecting at age 65 and you lived to be 95? You would have received $963,990 and again, you only deposited $275,000. That is three and a half times more money than you initially deposited.

But you may not live to be 95. The proverbial bus may hit you and your spouse, when you are 71, just five years into your retirement. How much will your heirs receive? First, let's calculate how much money you received. Based on the figures above, you were paid $160,665. To calculate your heir's forthcoming check, we have to peek back at the **accumulation account**. If good fortune was on your side, and the account grew to $531,882 as illustrated above, then they get a check for the difference between this and the amount you already spent. In other words, $531,882 - $160,665 = $371,217 for your grateful heirs. On the other hand, in the worst case scenario in which your actual account only grew at the rock bottom 1.25 percent, the math would look like this: $336,284 - $160,665 = $175,619. As my dad, Dale Stillman, was fond of saying, "Those are no small potatoes."

When you do the math, it's easy to see why boomers like this new hybrid / savings strategy. Sometimes people will ask me, "Hey, can I just buy the income rider without investing in the fixed index annuity?" The answer is, "No." Income riders are like sidecars on motorcycles. They are both headed to the same destination, but without the motorcycle the sidecar (income rider) isn't going anywhere.

Income riders aren't free, but they will not cost you an arm or a leg. Generally the cost is less than 1 percent. Some plans also offer a long term care rider that will double or triple your monthly check. This can be a viable option for people who didn't plan for long term care. I'm not going to go into a lot of detail here, but know that other options are available that may fill in some of the gaps in your retirement plan. Most importantly though, remember this: Annuities have lots of moving parts and this is one area where you owe it to yourself to work with a retirement planning specialist so you can get the best product to meet your needs. That having been said, this product is not for everyone. So maybe the best investment for you is not even an annuity. Get the facts and get qualified help before you make a decision.

A Retirement Income Planning Gem

It is my professional opinion that, in most situations, hybrid / fixed index annuities can be of tremendous benefit when planning for retirement. They provide safety, a fair rate of growth, guaranteed lifetime income (even with inflation protection), and long term care benefits or death benefits if needed. Not taking the time to learn more about how hybrid annuity strategies work is a serious mistake in my opinion. Our clients here at JDS Wealth Management Corp. have been taking advantage of these products for many years, and they have served us well in good times and bad.

If there is one thing you can glean from reading this book it's this: take the time to learn about Hybrid / Fixed Indexed Annuities! Don't miss out. If you decide they are not for you, fine. But at least you will have made an informed decision. Also, don't expect your broker or broker/dealer to understand these products, or recommend them. It is not what they do. They don't really understand them, and in most cases, the broker-dealer won't allow the sale of fixed indexed annuities because they are not a security (that means they're safe). Therefore, they will not promote them whether it is in your best interest or not. Wow! I guess I was pretty blunt there. But the truth is the truth and it has its own license to speak. It is what it is, as they say.

This is one reason we operate as an "Independent Registered Investment Advisory" firm and only operate on the "Institutional Wealth Management" level. No broker-dealer ever dictates what we sell to our clients or consumers in general. That is what being a fiduciary is all about – putting the interest of the client in first place. We make available countless studies, information, and reports documenting the successful results enjoyed by those who use Hybrid Fixed Index Annuity strategies in their income planning. All you have to do is contact us at (704) 660-0214, or email us at JDS Wealth Management and we'll gladly pass the information along.

A Word about Variable Annuities

Like all annuities, variable annuities are insurance products issued by various insurance companies. They're distributed through broker-dealer networks across the country. I'm going to be frank once again - I'm not a big fan of variable annuities for most people in retirement. Why? The two biggest reasons are risk, and fees.

Variable annuities invest in what's known as "sub-accounts". When you buy a variable annuity, you are essentially buying a mutual fund through an insurance company, with a death benefit wrapper. Mutual funds are risky, period. I know there are less risky mutual funds that can be diversified, blah, blah, blah. But, you can't diversify away what we call "systemic risk". Investments are either contractually guaranteed, or they're not. On variable annuities, death benefit and income riders can be purchased for a fee. That leads me to fees. It's typical to see variable annuities that have fees in excess of 3-4 percent!

Fees such as mortality and expense fees, death benefit fees, management fees, trading fees, administration fees, agent commission trails are all there draining your bottom line. Sometimes you have to get out your magnifying glass or search through the prospectus to find them, but they are there. The income riders in most cases can't compete with fixed index annuity income riders and many require annuitization to receive income. That means you lose control of your money if you turn on income. If you don't mind risk and you are a little younger, and you are willing to put up with the higher fees to get the greater upside potential for growth, then maybe a variable annuity can work for you. But I am not going to spend time explaining the pros and cons of variable annuities because I simply don't think they are a good "retirement planning" tool. I believe there are better annuity options in retirement than variable annuities. I know I just made a bunch of stock junkies and brokers really mad, but so be it. That's my story and I'm sticking to it!

Annuity Wrap Up

In my opinion, annuities should be a part of most retirement income plans. Why? It's really very simple. Annuities are the ONLY investment vehicle that can provide lifetime guaranteed income, period. In other words, look at them as your own personal family pension.

The trick is figuring out what type of annuity planning is right for you, and how to properly do it. Annuities have changed drastically over the years, and very few financial planners, brokers, bankers, etc. have an in depth knowledge and understanding of how to properly blend annuities into an overall retirement strategy. Annuities are like any other investment tool in the tool box. Some are good, some are bad. What's right for you might not be right for the folks next door. When you think annuity, think income, think pension. That's what annuities should be used for, INCOME. So, don't discount them because your broker wants you in the market forever, and don't fall overly in love with them either, just because that's all your insurance guy talks about. DO YOUR HOMEWORK! I'd also recommend working with an "Independent RIA" firm to help you with annuity decisions.

Chapter Eleven

Smooth Sailing Through The Golden Years

    In Chapter Six of this book I told you about my first "retirement" when my wife, Judy, and I took two years off when we were in our early thirties and sailed our 35-foot sloop, *Second Wind*, from the Great Lakes to the East Coast, Martha's Vinyard, Florida, the Keys, the Bahamas and back. On some days our voyage took us through storms and angry waves that pounded our bow and rattled our nerves. Then there were those glorious days when we had smooth sailing in calm waters, bright sun and dependable 12-knot winds. The weather was beautiful on one afternoon when we left Beaufort Inlet in North Carolina, our bow pointed south, riding over gentle 2-foot swells with a fine northwest wind across our starboard stern quarter – perfect for a comfortable broad reach down the coast. The thing about the eastern seaboard is that once you are clear of the North Carolina Outer Banks, the coastline takes a pronounced curve back westward, tempting southbound sailors to steer a straight course through the sometimes turbulent open Atlantic instead of taking the more placid Intracoastal Waterway.

    The Intracoastal Waterway is a serpentine 3,000-mile inland "river" that meanders down the east coast. It is a hodgepodge of dredged canals, natural lakes, creeks, saltwater rivers, bays, sounds and inlets. Boats of all sizes and descriptions use the ICW going both north and south between Massachusetts and Texas. The upside to taking the "ditch," as boaters have dubbed it, is that you are always in calm water. The downside, especially for a sailing vessel, is that you encounter several bascule and turnstile bridges that take their sweet time opening for you. Then there is also the shallow waters and tides that can run you aground if you aren't paying attention. The upside to the "ditch" is that you dodge the potential hazards of the sometimes manic Atlantic.

We plotted a course that would take us from Beaufort inlet to Masonboro Inlet, just north of Wilmington, North Carolina. As daylight faded, we were experiencing some of the most pleasant sailing since leaving Lake Michigan. *Second Wind* was loping along at a respectable seven knots in calm seas thanks to an offshore breeze. After sundown, however, the wind began to shift. The full moon we had been using to steer by began ducking behind thickening clouds. The gentle swells turned in to a medium to heavy chop which jabbed at our bow as we pinched into a brisk headwind. Intermittent showers peppered the cockpit. We may have saved a little time, but it was hardly worth the rough ride. I can't remember a more welcome sight or sound than the flashing light on the noisy whistle buoy that marks the entrance to Masonboro Inlet and the calm water of the ICW which lay beyond.

Finding smooth sailing in retirement is largely a matter of making right decisions and staying on course. Had we consulted the weather more closely instead of relying on our own impulses we could have avoided a miserable night at sea. By consulting a financial advisor who is a qualified retirement income specialist you avoid inordinate risk and overpayment of taxes. You may also save thousands of dollars for yourself in retirement and establish a legacy for those you leave behind. What follows are just a few examples of strategies that are by no means secret. I share them with you here to make the point that, just as you are prudent to seek the advice of a guide when traveling in unfamiliar territory, you are wise to seek the advice of a trained financial professional to avoid tax traps and other hazards that may present themselves in your retirement.

Avoiding the "Senior Only" Tax

The story goes that when Franklin D. Roosevelt signed the Social Security Act in to law in 1935 reporters asked him if these benefits would be taxed. He is reported to have slammed his fist down on the desk in the Oval Office and vowed that he would never tax Social Security benefits. But during Ronald Reagan's presidency the Social

Security Amendments of 1983 changed the rules allowing for up to 50 percent of your Social Security benefits to be taxed if your annual income exceeded 25,000 as a single filer or $32,000 per year as a married couple filing jointly.

A 1993 adjustment when Bill Clinton was president allowed for taxation on up to 85 percent of benefits for single filers earning more than $34,000 and couples earning $44,000 or more. So it's not uncommon for new retirees to discover that they are in a higher tax bracket than they anticipated and learn to their chagrin that they have to pay taxes. Others aren't surprised; they just shrug and pay, as if to say, "Oh well, Uncle Sam giveth and Uncle Sam taketh away."

But it doesn't necessarily have to be that way if you do a little planning with a competent financial advisor. There are strategies that in some cases can reduce and even perhaps eliminate Social Security taxes. Remember, taxes on Social Security benefits are based on how much **reportable income** you earn each year. Reportable income includes (if not an IRA / Qualified Account):

- Investment income from stocks, mutual funds, etc.
- Pension income
- CD and other income from banks
- Tax-free municipal bond income (surprised?)
- 50 percent of Social Security income in some cases

How do you find out where you stand? If you file as an individual and your combined income — by this, Social Security means adjusted gross income and nontaxable interest plus one-half of your Social Security benefits — is below $25,000, your benefits won't be taxed at all. If income is between $25,000 and $34,000, up to half of your benefits may be subject to tax. For income of more than $34,000, up to 85 percent of your benefits may be considered taxable income.

If you and your spouse file a joint return with a combined income below $32,000, your benefits are out of reach. For income between $32,000 and $44,000, up to 50 percent of benefits may be taxable, and up to 85 percent if combined income is more than $44,000.

One perfectly legal and acceptable (to the IRS) to avoid over taxation is to simply place a portion of your assets in tax-deferred accounts, where the interest received is not considered reportable income by the IRS. Like what? For one, gains paid on annuity balances are tax deferred and are not considered "reportable" income on form 1040. This is not the case with CDs and gains from mutual funds. Those gains are fully reportable. So, if gains from CDs and Mutual Funds are putting you over the taxation threshold, then the solution is obvious. Move the money. Sure, you will *eventually* pay taxes on annuity gains, but the more income you can move to the *unreportable* side of the tax return form, the further away you stand from Social Security Taxation.

I advise anyone considering making such changes to consult with a tax professional first. This is because every case is different and the tax professional is able to inform you accurately as to whether such a move is in compliance and is in your best interest. But here is a practical illustration:

If Rick, a single tax payer receives $12,000 per year in Social Security benefits, plus $10,000 in taxable interest, plus $10,000 in tax-free interest, plus $5000 in IRA distributions, he will have to pay taxes on $3000 of his Social Security. Rick can expect, on average, to fork over $750 to Uncle Sam. If nothing changes, he may be doing this for the next 20 years. That will add up to $15,000 which Rick could have used to pay for trips to the beach, private pilot lessons, or even the simple pleasure of eating out more often. Worst case, Rick could have dropped that chunk of change into the coffer of his favorite charity (I doubt the U.S. government tops his list of favorite charities).

But what happens if Rick consults a professional and does a little planning, and by moving some of his assets into tax-deferred investments reduces his taxable interest to $5,000? None of his social security is subject to tax and he avoids paying $750 in taxes.

1099 Reportable Income AKA "Phantom Income"

A qualified financial planner specializing in retirement income planning will be able to help you identify phantom income – that is income that is reported to the IRS on your behalf, but you that you never actually receive. An example would be when your mutual fund manager buys or sells stocks within the fund at a profit. Though you never see the money from this activity, you are responsible for the taxes. If this is a problem in your current retirement portfolio, repositioning your assets can eliminate or perhaps minimize your tax liability.

Stretching Your IRA

Most people don't mind paying their fair share of taxes. They just don't want to pay *more* than their fair share. Certain tax rules allow you to position an IRA so that you can create a legacy for future generations while protecting them from burdensome and unfair taxes. I have seen some situations where the IRS legitimately claims as much as 60-80 percent of an IRA inheritance when a little planning could have prevented it.

Without planning scenario - A husband leaves an IRA to his wife. She takes ownership as her own IRA. Then a few years later she dies. By now the account is worth $250,000. She leaves it to her son, Rodney, who makes $50,000 per year. Rodney is notified by the custodians of the IRA that they are sending him a check for a quarter of a million dollars! To this point no taxes have been paid on any of this money. So when Rodney inherits $250,000, it is added to his income as if he earned it on the job that year. He is catapulted into the highest tax bracket. Do you see a problem developing here? Rodney may have to pay as much as 40-50 percent of the $250,000, or $100,000 to the IRS in ordinary income tax! As of this writing the highest federal income tax rate is 39.6 percent (and on the way up), the Affordable Care Act adds another 3.8 percent for a single filer that earns over $200k, and whatever state tax applies wherever you live. Ouch!

With planning scenario - Rodney's parents had a financial advisor who understood Publication 590 in the IRS code. They made their IRA a multi-generational, or stretch IRA – so called because the tax-deferred status of the IRA is stretched out to future generations for decades to come, avoiding the taxes caused if taking the distribution upfront. They named Rodney and his children as specific beneficiaries, which enabled each generation to take annual distributions according to their life expectancy. Rodney avoids the big tax bite.

Meanwhile, the money in the IRA grows at compound interest, tax deferred. He is able to leave it to his children. They are able to take distributions over the course of their lifetimes. The IRA continues to grow, benefiting both Rodney and his family.

Key requirements for Stretch IRAs:

- A stretch IRA has to be properly named and titled.
- The beneficiaries have to be properly named and titled.
- Make sure that your IRA is placed with a company that will allow and execute stretch IRA options. ***Note: Not all companies or custodians will allow for stretch IRA options! You must make sure your custodian will allow this, and make sure you read the "custodial documents."***

If all of this sounds a little detailed, it is because it is. No one wants to find out later that they left one "t" uncrossed and it spoiled the whole plan – especially when the penalty can be hundreds of thousands of dollars. That's why you should seek the help of a financial advisor who knows how the moving parts of this strategy work.

Knowledge Is Power?

These are just a couple of strategies that can make a big difference in your retirement. There are many more but time does not allow me to cover them all in this book.

Once in a philosophy class, an inquisitive student raised his hand and asked the seasoned professor a deep question: "What is the difference between knowledge, understanding and wisdom?"

The room grew quiet. After scratching his chin for a moment, the professor replied, "Let me explain it this way. Let's say you are standing on a railroad track. You have ***knowledge*** of the fact that the train is coming.

The class nodded, paying rapt attention, expecting more. The professor, grasping his lapels, continued:

"You comprehend the relationship between the hard steel of the locomotive and the soft tissue of your limbs - that's ***understanding.***"

The class leaned forward expectantly.

"Wisdom," said the professor, "would be getting off the track!"

The old expression "knowledge is power," is not exactly accurate in my opinion. Knowledge is only power when it is applied. Knowledge, for example, is the accumulation of facts. The man on the railroad track was collecting all kinds of knowledge as he stood there observing the train coming at him. He had already collected a fund of knowledge about physics and the law of inertia, gravity, and understood all the science associated with force. He even had a rudimentary medical knowledge – at least enough to know that physical harm (read instant death) would result were he to be hit by the fast-approaching locomotive. All that knowledge, however, would not have benefited him one whit had he not applied it. *Applying that knowledge, however, would require him to get off the tracks! In other words, "Applied Knowledge" Is Power!*

Afterword

As I mentioned early on in this book, my main objective is to educate and motivate. If I have done those to some small degree then it is mission accomplished for me.

On one of the first sail boats I owned, the mechanism connecting the wooden tiller in the cockpit to the rudder below broke. One minute I was steering the boat toward the marina and the next minute the tiller moved freely but the boat did not respond. As I would later discover, a small clamp had come loose and it was a simple repair to make once in port. But to get there, for a short time I had to sail without a rudder. That meant I had to steer the boat by balancing the sails to the wind perfectly, hoping no one got in my way! I got the anchor ready so that when we got close to the marina, I could set the hook and secure our position before we got into even more trouble by crashing into other boats, or the rock covered breakwater. While this was going on, I was hoping my good friend who I had called on the marine band radio, was on his way to tow me safely in.

Fortunately for me, the wind held steady and the anchor held firm when we needed it. My friend showed up right on cue, and towed us into our marina slip without incident. One thing I learned from that experience is that a boat without a rudder is like a log in the water. You are at the mercy of the wind and the tides, and it pays to be prepared.

I am still surprised at how many people are rudderless when it comes to financial planning. They let life happen to them, financially speaking, instead of taking steps to control their financial future. I hope that some of the information you have gleaned from this book will be useful to you in taking control of your financial life and enable you to set sail, so to speak, to the great retirement destination that you deserve… **without the burden of stress and worry.**

There is no better feeling than to know that you are in control of your future but there are many things about life we simply can't control. All the financial knowledge and wisdom in the world will not prevent the next market crash, any more than a world congress of meteorologists can stop a storm at sea. But what we CAN do is prepare for contingencies to the extent of our capability. Like the ancient adage, "we may not be able to control the wind, but we can adjust our sails".

A Few of My Final Thoughts

Going through the process of writing this book has been a cathartic experience for me. It has allowed me to reflect on my life and upbringing. It has made me realize how lucky I am to have been raised by wonderful parents who had good "old fashion" Midwestern values". We were never "rich" moneywise, but we always had what we needed.

I was fortunate to have a wonderful childhood that taught me the value of honesty, family, friendship, and caring for others. My father engrained in me at a young age to be good at whatever you do. He used to say, "If you're going to half ass it, don't do it at all"! My grandfather always said, "don't be a jack of all trades, master of none". I guess that's why I've always tried to excel at whatever I've attempted to do and have always believed that if you give it 100% and try your best with integrity, things will work out for the best.

In summary, here are a few things I think are crucial when it comes to retirement planning.

- A) Don't take on more risk than is necessary in retirement. Wall Street can be your best friend, or your worst enemy, especially in retirement.
- B) Focus on preservation of assets, and **_guaranteed income planning_** once retired. Your income will dictate your lifestyle, and guarantee your independence in retirement. Chasing performance is a very dangerous thing for us old folks!
- C) Take the time to learn about new **_hybrid strategies_** for annuities, life insurance, and long term care. These newer hybrid strategies have been designed for the baby boom generation, and are very beneficial when used properly. You need to speak to an "Independent Registered Investment Advisor" to learn about these strategies. Don't

expect your broker to understand or tell you about these opportunities, it's not what they do, and they ***can't*** promote them.

D) Take the time to learn about "Institutional Wealth Management" investing. Work with an "Independent Registered Investment Advisor" that has a "Fiduciary" responsibility. This allows you to get the best advice, is 100 percent transparent, and will lower overall fees.

E) Have a long term care plan! LTC will be one of the biggest liabilities in your retirement. It can destroy your estate, and if you're age 65 and over, you have a 70 percent chance that will happen. Stop procrastinating! There are alternatives to traditional long term care insurance. We've discussed a few in this book. Please seek out the advice of a professional in this area.

F) Have proper legal documents in place. Everyone should have a will, a living will, general / durable power of attorney, and healthcare power of attorney at the bare minimum. These are simple documents that can, and will protect your estate.

These items are all critical to planning your retirement, and protecting your estate for loved ones. If you don't mind, let me be very blunt once more. This stuff is really important right? So, it's very simple. If you have not done these six things, get your head out of the sand, stop procrastinating, and do it! As my father always said to us kids, "did I make myself clear"?

About the Author

James D. "Jim" Stillman grew up in Milwaukee, Wisconsin which is listed as the second coldest large city in the lower 48 states. But the warmth of Jim's family was constant and abiding. His mother, Doris Stillman, had three children of her own but she always made room for foster children when Jim was growing up.

"She had the biggest heart of anyone I've ever known," Jim said, "and she taught her children to be generous, respectful, caring adults. Jim's family adopted one of the foster children they cared for, growing their family to four children. The adopted foster child was named Theresa.

Jim says, "I'll never forget how my father fought with the judge for the right to adopt Theresa". Typically foster children are given to adoptive parents once they are found, and the foster parents must give up the child at some point. But, after having Theresa for approximately five years, Jim's parents were having none of that!

"She was now a part of our family," Jim explained. "My dad stood face to face with the judge and told him, 'If you want to take my daughter away from us you'll have to go through me first!'" The family stood together, and the court system and judge agreed that the best thing for Theresa was to remain a part of the Stillman family.

Jim grew up observing how his industrious father, Dale Stillman, worked two jobs to support his large family. As soon as Jim was old enough to hold the handle of a shovel he was earning money removing snow from driveways and sidewalks. In the summer he mowed lawns, delivered newspapers and worked on his grandparents' dairy farm. When Jim entered high school, he became a lifeguard on Lake Michigan for the Milwaukee County Lifeguard program in the summers.

"My dad was a bit of a perfectionist," says Jim with a smile. "He would always say, 'If you are not going to do it right, then don't do it at all!' So I learned early to pay attention to detail and do things the right way.'"

Owing to his ability to repair almost anything, Jim's father was lovingly known as "Mr. Fix-it" by neighbors. He was especially gifted when it came to repairing small engines, and tuning up cars.

Jim learned industry, thrift and the value of being honest from his parents, and grandparents. "I never worked as hard as I did when I worked on Grandpa's dairy farm, "say's Jim. He recounted some of the valuable lessons his grandfather left with him, the most memorable of which was "Your word is your bond and your handshake is a personal guarantee."

Jim says he learned to sail at the age of 16 on Pike Lake just outside of Hartford, Wisconsin, which is about an hour or so north of Milwaukee. Every Sunday was spent on the water sailing small, fast scows. "I fell in love with the movement and the exhilaration of being moved by the wind," says Jim. "Twenty miles per hour doesn't sound like a lot, but that's fast on the water."

Jim's first career was in the printing industry in the early 1970s. Business was good, and Jim earned two apprenticeships becoming a journeyman printer and color artist. Jim's wife Judy is a registered nurse. Together they worked hard, budgeted, and saved enough to "retire" for two years while they were in their early 30s. They fulfilled a lifelong dream by sailing their 35' sailboat, "Second Wind," through the Great Lakes, Erie Barge Canal System to the east coast, through Long Island Sound, and up to Martha's Vinyard. From there they sailed down the east coast to Florida, cutting through the Ocheechobee Waterway to Fort Myers, then up the gulf to Clearwater, Florida, to visit good friends. Then it was on to the Keys, and Bahamas and back. Jim says that experience changed their lives forever as a young couple. "It broadened our horizons, and taught us life lessons at a young age," he says.

Jim and Judy have two children, a son Tyler and a daughter, Kelly, who now works with Jim at JDS Enterprizes Inc. and JDS Wealth Management Corp., a Registered Investment Advisory firm Jim founded after the family moved to North Carolina. When asked about the decision to move south, Jim says that while on their sailing journey he and Judy discussed the merits of every place they visited as a possible place to eventually live. "In my ships log, I wrote more about the Carolina coast than anywhere else," says Jim. "We fell in love with the state, the people, the weather, and the fact that you are just a few hours away from both the mountains and the ocean."

About his decision to enter the financial advisory profession, Jim says that he was influenced by a friend who was a financial advisor. This came about after the company Jim worked for was sold, and he decided to move on to another profession.

"My friend told me about how much he was able to help people at the critical moment of their lives when they entered retirement," Jim said. "I have always been a people person and the idea of doing something as meaningful as that appealed to me." I also would have the opportunity to build my own business, and be in control of my own destiny Jim says.

Following his father's advice to "do it right or don't do it at all," Jim began taking the courses and obtaining the licenses required to become a financial advisor. In 2003 he founded JDS Enterprizes Inc., and founded JDS Wealth Management Corporation in 2008. Jim and his daughter Kelly, also host a weekly radio talk show about retirement planning called "The Safe Harbor Retirement Planning Show". Jim writes a monthly educational article in "Lake Norman Magazine," and has been honored as one of the Charlotte area's top Five-Star wealth managers.

In addition to being the CEO / President and founder of JDS Wealth Management Corp., Jim is both a Registered Investment Advisor (RIA) and an Investment Advisor Representative (IAR), has obtained his Series 65, 63 & 6 licenses with the SEC (Securities and Exchange Commission). Jim is also a Registered Financial Consultant (RFC), and a member of the Financial Planning Association. He also holds his Life & Health, as well as his Medicare and Long Term Care licenses for insurance planning.

James can be reached at james@jdswealthmanagement.com or by calling 704-660-0214.

Dedication

    This book is dedicated to my wife Judy, without whose endless support I could not have accomplished the things in life we've been fortunate enough to accomplish. She is my best friend, my foundation. She is the compass that guides me through life. Without her, I'd be a rudderless ship at sea. To my children, Kelly and Tyler, who have grown to be respectful, caring adults and have stayed out of trouble and help run the business. Also to my mother, Doris Stillman who was always my biggest cheerleader and made me believe I could accomplish anything I set my mind to. She taught me to have a kind heart and to respect and help others. To this day, I have never met anyone with a caring heart the size of my Mom's. And to my father, Dale Stillman, who taught me the value of hard work, giving it your all, honesty and integrity, and the sobering truth that it takes a lifetime to build trust and only one day to tear it down. And lastly, to my grandparents Florence and Frank Stillman who again taught me the value of hard work, honesty, and integrity. Those summers spent working on my grandparent's dairy farm were hard work to say the least, but as I've grown older I now see just how valuable that experience was.

    I'm very fortunate to have a loving, caring, supportive family. I can't express in words how much I love and appreciate you guys, and everyone who's ever assisted me in attaining my personal goals in life. Thank you!

Acknowledgements

I would like to express my gratitude to the many people who saw me through this project to help me shape my observations and opinions for this book.

I would especially like to thank my copy editor and co-author Tom Bowen, for helping me crystallize my focus and get the book from mind into print and ready for publishing. Thank you Tom, I'm honored to consider you my friend and co-author.

I appreciate the valuable assistance of Advisors Excel, and the Advisors Excel Creative Services team for the design, coordination, and implementation of all the pieces that were put together to create this book. Thank you Advisors Excel for your support.

I'd like to send out a special thank you to my first mentor, and good friend Frank Tebyani. When I first started out in this business, Frank took me under his wing and made sure I'd be successful. Thanks Frank, I'll always appreciate how you stood by me, were always there for support, and how you always motivated me no matter how tough learning the business got from time to time.

I also want to acknowledge my good friend and mentor Tom McDermott. When I decided to become an "Independent Agent" and go into business for myself, Tom was my mentor in that journey. I'll have to admit, it was really scary to go out on my own. Tom was there every step of the way, guiding me, teaching me, supporting me, and giving me proven systems of success to use. Tom, I'll always be grateful for your support and friendship. You and your organization changed my life, and gave me the confidence to move onward and upward in the financial services profession and expand my horizons. Even when I decided to move on to other challenges, and to another organization, Tom treated me with respect and encouragement. I'll always be grateful for Tom's professionalism. Tom is a "class act", and I'm fortunate to call him my mentor and friend.

Lastly, I want to thank all of our wonderful clients at JDS Wealth Management Corp., and JDS Enterprizes Inc. who have put their faith in us. We appreciate the opportunity to serve you, and cherish the friendships we've been fortunate to build. Thank you for your trust in our firm.

www.ingramcontent.com/pod-product-compliance
Lightning Source LLC
Chambersburg PA
CBHW051714170526
45167CB00002B/661